Cambridge Primary Path

Foundation

Student's Book

Kim Milne

CAMBRIDGE UNIVERSITY PRESS

LEVEL F: Scope and Sequence

1 Big Question: Who am I?

Reading	Vocabulary	Grammar
Nonfiction *We Are All Different!* **Reading Strategy** Similarities and Differences **Fiction** *Grandma Turtle* **Reading Strategy** Real or Fantasy?	**Key Words 1:** favorite, color, hair, girl, brown, boy **Key Words 2:** short, long, tall, curly, straight, blond **Key Words 3:** class, different **Key Words 4:** old, slow, fast, tired, young, happy	**Verb *to be*: Affirmative and Negative** I am six years old. I'm not tall. He is short. She isn't short. **Verb *to be*: Affirmative and Negative** You are young. You aren't old. They are happy. They aren't slow.

2 Big Question: What is school?

Reading	Vocabulary	Grammar
Nonfiction *Welcome to My School* **Reading Strategy** Classifying **Fiction** *I Can't Find My Things!* **Reading Strategy** Understanding a Character's Feelings	**Key Words 1:** desk, teacher, classroom, gym, bathroom, playground **Key Words 2:** library, schoolbag, pencil case, notebook, colored pencil, eraser **Key Words 3:** classmates, apple **Key Words 4:** story, sad, mad, hungry, lunchbox, surprised	***a / an*** a pencil an eraser **Possessive Adjectives** This is your desk. It is his first day at school. I can't find my book. Gemma shares her pencils with Max.

3 Big Question: What is a toy?

Reading	Vocabulary	Grammar
Nonfiction *Top Five Toys* **Reading Strategy** Classifying Words **Fiction** *Don't Touch!* **Reading Strategy** Ordering Story Events	**Key Words 1:** toy, box, house, paper, airplane, tablet **Key Words 2:** robot, fun, dollhouse, tent, train, jump rope **Key Words 3:** jump, children **Key Words 4:** monkey bars, bike, car, action figure, dinosaur, spaceship	**Commands** Listen! March! Stop! Stand! Sit! Jump! **Negative Commands** Don't touch my cars! Don't run!

4 Big Question: What makes a home?

Reading	Vocabulary	Grammar
Nonfiction *All Kinds of Homes* **Reading Strategy** Comparing **Fiction** *Snail Finds His Home* **Reading Strategy** Plot and Setting	**Key Words 1:** home, family, dining room, living room, bedroom, kitchen **Key Words 2:** apartment, room, water, garden, stove, bed **Key Words 3:** roof, stairs **Key Words 4:** snail, ladybug, forest, spider, butterfly, mouse	**Prepositions** It's in the kitchen. It's on the roof. It's under the tree house. **Verb *to be*: *Yes/No* Questions (Singular)** Is Mouse under a tree? No, he isn't. He's in a hole. Is Spider under the leaf? Yes, he is.

5 Big Question: Where do wild animals belong?

Reading	Vocabulary	Grammar
Nonfiction *Top Five Wild Animals* **Reading Strategy** Visualizing **Fiction** *The Rabbit on the Moon* **Reading Strategy** Predicting from Pictures	**Key Words 1:** zebra, land, elephant, octopus, ocean, dolphin **Key Words 2:** teeth, tail, beak, jungle, claw, fur **Key Words 3:** feathers, insects **Key Words 4:** rabbit, moon, snake, tongue, sun, stars	**Verb *to be*: *Wh–* Questions** What color are they? They are black and white. What are they? They're baby pandas. **Verb *to be*: *Yes/No* Questions (Plural)** Are Ketzi and the little rabbit near the stars? Yes, they are. / No, they aren't.

Oracy Skill	Phonics	Ready to Write	Listening	The Big Challenge	Speaking Mission
Ground Rules Listen to others. Take turns. Respect others. Share your ideas. Raise your hand to speak. **Cue Card:** 1 This is …	**The Alphabet**	**Learn to Write** Capital and Lowercase Letters	**Dialogue** Talking About Your Favorite Thing	**How can we talk about ourselves?**	**Saying Who You Are When You Are Lost**

Oracy Skill	Phonics	Ready to Write	Listening	The Big Challenge	Speaking Mission
Agreeing and Disagreeing **Cue Cards:** 2 Yes. 3 No.	**Initial Sounds** *c, p, t, n, b, h*	**Learn to Write** Alphabetical Order	**Song** Describing Your School	**How can we make a classroom map?**	**Borrowing Something at School**

Oracy Skill	Phonics	Ready to Write	Listening	The Big Challenge	Oracy Task
Active Listening **Cue Card:** 4 Please repeat that.	**Ending Sounds:** *-at, -en*	**Learn to Write** Complete Sentences	**Dialogue** Playing a Game	**How can we make a toy?**	**Collaboration** Agreeing on Buying a Toy

Oracy Skill	Phonics	Ready to Write	Listening	The Big Challenge	Speaking Mission
Taking Turns **Cue Cards:** 5 It's my turn. 6 It's your turn.	**Ending Sounds:** *-ut, -ig*	**Learn to Write** Nouns	**Poem** What Home Means to You	**How can I describe my home?**	**Describing an Object You Lost**

Oracy Skill	Phonics	Ready to Write	Listening	The Big Challenge	Speaking Mission
Participating Actively **Cue Card:** 7 Let's …	**Initial Sounds:** *q, s, f, j, g, r*	**Learn to Write** Identify Questions and Exclamations	**Guessing Game** Identifying Wild Animals	**How can we describe a wild animal?**	**Playing a Board Game**

LEVEL F: Scope and Sequence

6 Big Question: What can people do?

Reading	Vocabulary	Grammar
Nonfiction *Kids with Amazing Abilities* **Reading Strategy** Predicting from Titles **Fiction** *Hip-hop Hanna* **Reading Strategy** Cause and Effect	**Key Words 1:** ability, paint, run, skate, play basketball, talk **Key Words 2:** see, ride, climb, say, spell, swim **Key Words 3:** blind, backwards **Key Words 4:** music, love, dancer, practice, read, puppy	***I can / I can't*** I **can ride** a horse. I **can't walk**. ***Yes/No* Questions with *can* and *can't*** **Can** Hanna **dance** well? **Yes, she can.** **No, she can't.**

7 Big Question: Is all food healthy?

Reading	Vocabulary	Grammar
Nonfiction *Snacks from Around the World!* **Reading Strategy** Similarities and Differences **Fiction** *No Broccoli, Please!* **Reading Strategy** Main Idea	**Key Words 1:** fruit, banana, grapes, vegetable, spinach, sugar **Key Words 2:** juice, water, oil, yogurt, tomato, rice **Key Words 3:** fried, freezer **Key Words 4:** broccoli, fish, French fries, chocolate, soup, muffin	***like / don't like*** I **like** peanut butter sandwiches. I **don't like** cheese sandwiches. ***Yes/No* Questions with *like*** **Do** you **like** broccoli now? **Yes, I do.** **No, I don't.**

8 Big Question: Are routines important?

Reading	Vocabulary	Grammar
Nonfiction *Henry's Healthy Habits* **Reading Strategy** Summarizing **Fiction** *Andy Ant* **Reading Strategy** Making Judgments	**Key Words 1:** brush my teeth, eat breakfast, go to school, walk, ride my bike, take the bus **Key Words 2:** sleep, do exercise, have fun, take a bath, change clothes, wash my hands **Key Words 3:** before, after **Key Words 4:** wake up, collect, march, find, carry, clean	**Present Simple: Affirmative** I **wash** my hands. I **sleep** 10 hours each night. **Present Simple: Negative** I **don't sleep** on Saturdays! We **don't work** on Saturdays.

9 Big Question: Why do we wear different clothes?

Reading	Vocabulary	Grammar
Nonfiction *Traditional Clothes from Around the World* **Reading Strategy** Cause and Effect **Fiction** *The Emperor's New Clothes* **Reading Strategy** Beginning, Middle, and End	**Key Words 1:** clothes, cold, jacket, hot, T-shirt, shoes **Key Words 2:** wear, hat, skirt, pants, gloves, dress **Key Words 3:** wool, cool **Key Words 4:** emperor, thief, palace, expensive, smart, fool	**Present Continuous: Affirmative and Negative** **I'm wearing** gloves and big boots. **I'm not wearing** a hat. **She's wearing** a long skirt. **He's not wearing** a jacket. **Present Continuous: *Yes/No* Questions** **Are** you **wearing** magic clothes? **Yes, I am.** **Are** you **wearing** your new clothes? **No, I'm not.**

Oracy Skill	Phonics	Ready to Write	Listening	The Big Challenge	Oracy Task
Asking for Agreement **Cue Cards:** 2 Yes. 3 No. 8 Do you agree?	**Initial Sounds:** *h, t, p, m, b, d*	**Learn to Write** Verbs	**Dialogue** Asking for Help	**What different things can we do?**	**Discussion** Agreeing on a Game to Play

Oracy Skill	Phonics	Ready to Write	Listening	The Big Challenge	Speaking Mission
Giving and Responding to Positive Feedback **Cue Cards:** 9 Good job! 10 Thank you.	**Ending Sounds:** *x, m, b*	**Learn to Write** Adjectives	**Song** Healthy Food vs. Junk Food	**How can we make a healthy dessert?**	**Buying Groceries**

Oracy Skill	Phonics	Ready to Write	Listening	The Big Challenge	Speaking Mission
Speaking Up **Cue Cards:** 4 Please repeat that. 11 I don't understand.	**Ending Sounds** *-sk, -st, -nt*	**Learn to Write** Statements	**Presentation** Talking About Morning and Bedtime Routines	**How can we describe our routines?**	**Assigning Tasks to Follow a Class Routine**

Oracy Skill	Phonics	Ready to Write	Listening	The Big Challenge	Oracy Task
Standing Up Straight and Keeping Still **Cue Cards:** 1 This is… 12 These are …	**Initial Sounds:** *gr- pl-*	**Learn to Write** Questions	**Presentation** Describing What You Wear	**How do we dress for special occasions?**	**Presentation** Giving a Final Presentation

What's Your Name?

1 0.1 Listen and number.

2 Get into a circle and ask each other's name.

3 Write your name on the board.

4 Write your name below.

I'm ______________________.

What Color Is It?

1 0.2 Sing and point.

2 Color and sing your song.

GREEN BLUE YELLOW

RED ORANGE PURPLE

Counting from 1 to 10

1 Write the missing numbers.

1	2		4	5
6		8	9	

2 0.3 Listen, point, and repeat.

3 0.4 Sing the song using your hands.

4 Now use colored pencils to count.

1 ONE	2 TWO	3 THREE	4 FOUR	5 FIVE
6 SIX	7 SEVEN	8 EIGHT	9 NINE	10 TEN

My Body

1 0.5 Follow the pictures and say the chant.

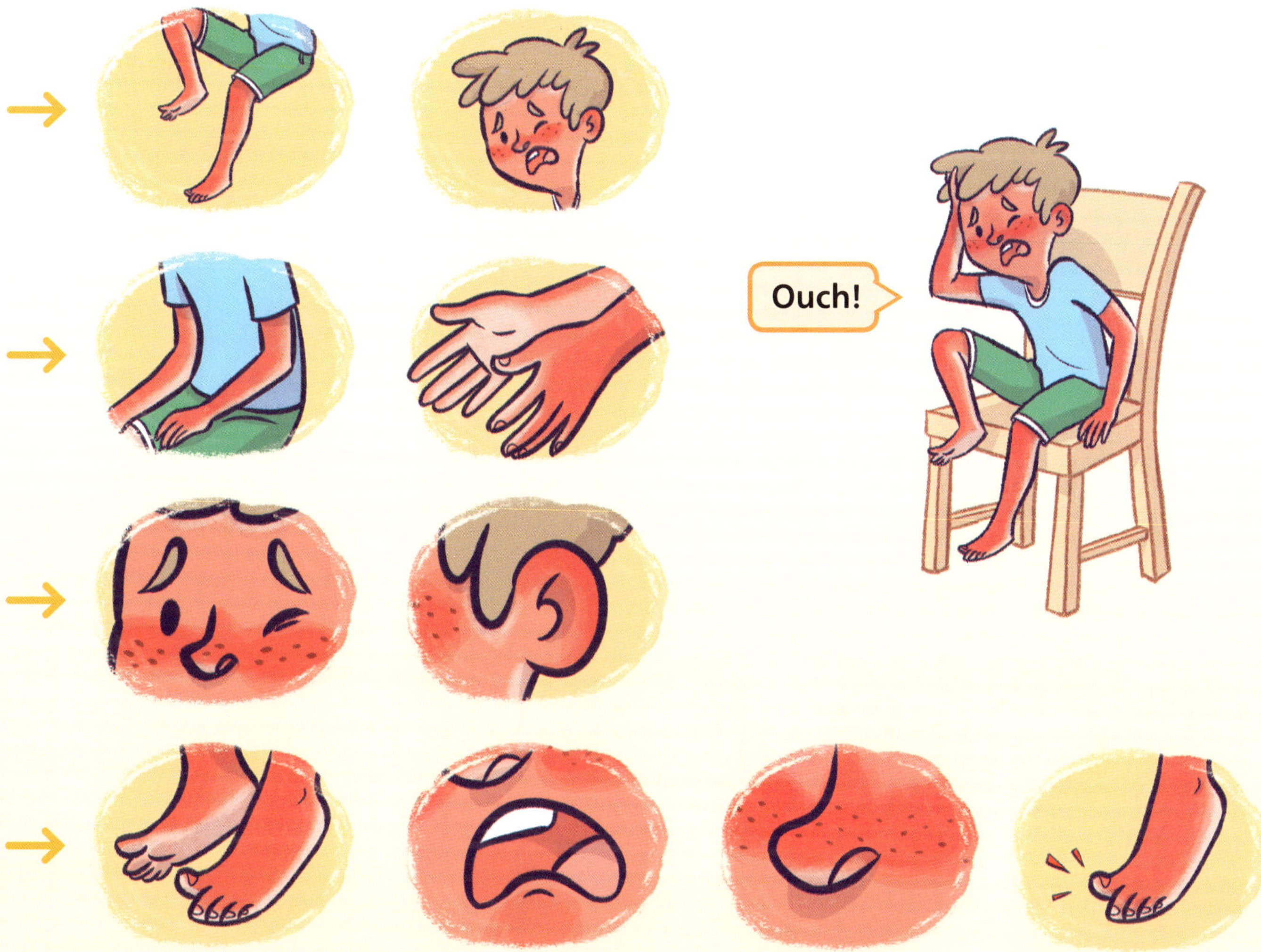

2 0.5 Listen again. Say the chant and act it out.

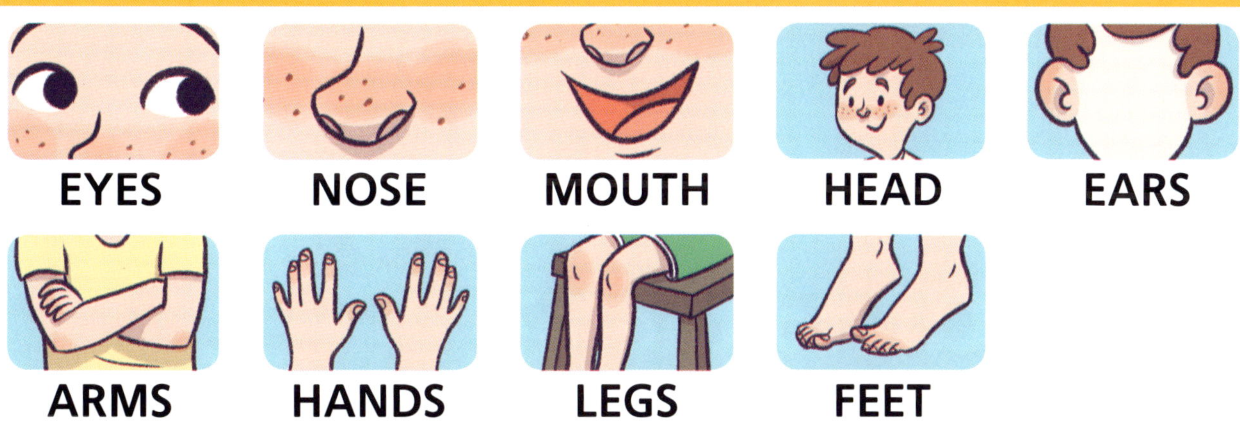

1 Who am I?

- ☐ **Describe** yourself.
- ☐ **Use** ground rules to work in groups.
- ☐ **Identify** capital and lowercase letters.
- ☐ **Talk** about yourself to the class.
- ☐ **Give** your personal information.

Who is a boy?

Who is a girl?

Are you similar to them?

Key Words 1

- favorite
- color
- hair
- girl
- brown
- boy

1 1.1 **Watch the video. Circle what is mentioned in the video.**

2 1.1 **Watch again. Complete the graphic organizer in the Activity Book.**

AB page 2

Ready to Read: Nonfiction

Reading Strategy: Similarities and Differences

1 🎧 1.2 Listen, point, and repeat.

eyes

hair

brown

orange

2 🎧 1.3 Listen and number the pictures.

a

b

c
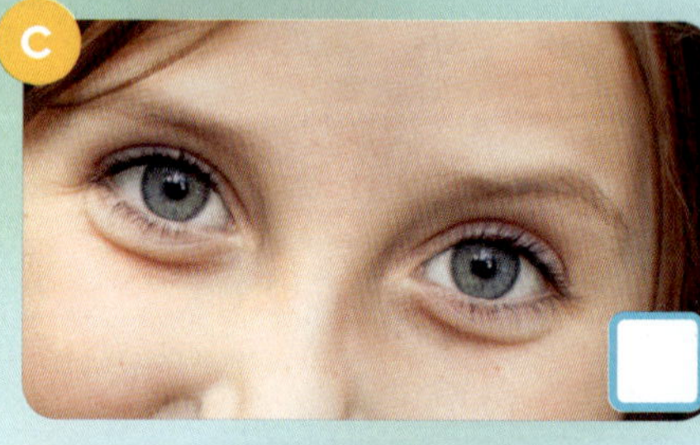

d

e

f

3 Are you similar to Larissa? Draw and color about yourself.

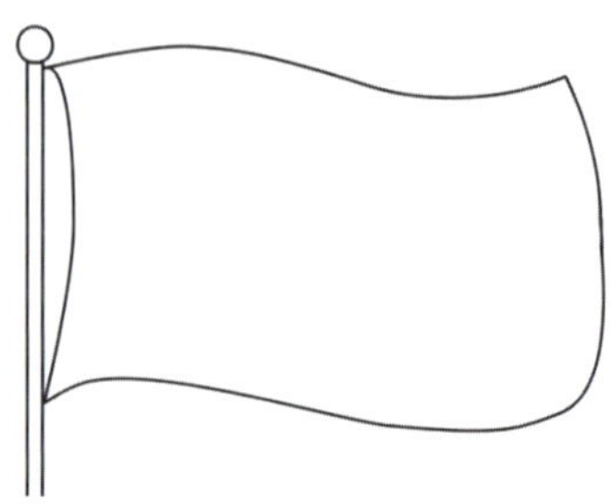

? Who are you?
I'm María. I'm from Spain.

1.4

Key Words 2

short

long

tall

curly

straight

blond

1.5

We Are All Different!

This is my class.
We are all different.

This is Onur.
He has black hair and brown eyes.
He's **short**.

1.6 We Are All Different!

This is Emily.
She has **long** hair.
She isn't short.
She's **tall**.

This is Diane.
She is seven years old.
She doesn't have **curly** hair. She has **straight** hair.

I'm Flora.
I'm six years old.
I have **blond** hair and blue eyes.
I'm not tall. I'm short.

Think

What are you like?

I have brown hair and green eyes.
I'm tall.

Explore the Text

1 Who is who? Write *E* for Emily, *D* for Diane, or *F* for Flora.

a

b
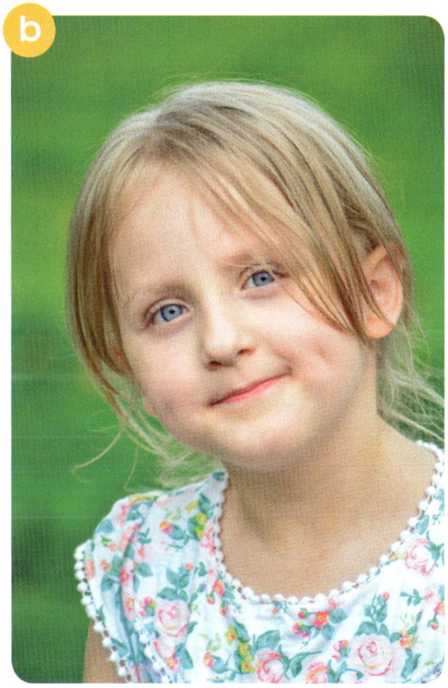

c

2 What are the similarities and differences between Emily, Diane, and Flora?

Flora has blond hair. Diane doesn't have blond hair. She has red hair.

3 1.7 Key Words 3 Listen and repeat. Number the pictures.

Time to Talk!

1 Draw your portrait.
2 Present your picture to the class.

I'm Tommy. I have brown hair and green eyes.

Grammar in Context

Grammar: Verb *to be*: Affirmative and Negative

I am six years old.	I'm not tall.
He is short.	She isn't short.

1 1.8 **Listen and draw the candles on the cakes.**

1 I am …

2 She is …

3 He is …

2 1.8 **Listen again and trace.**

1

I am five.

2

She is seven.

3

He is eight.

3 1.9 **Listen and say the chant.**

I'm tall. He's short.

I'm eight. He's six.

Blond hair. Black hair.

I have straight hair.

Time to Talk!

1 Write your age on a piece of paper.
2 Give it to a classmate.
3 Say your age and your classmate's age.

I'm six. She isn't six. She's five.

1 1.10 **Listen and sing.**

The Alphabet Song

2 1.10 **Trace the missing letters and sing again.**

A B C D

E F G

H I J K

L M N O P

Q R S T U V

W X Y Z

Time to Talk!

Spell your name.

I'm Baris.
B – A – R – I – S

3 **Play in pairs.**

a With your finger, write a letter on your partner's back.

b Your partner guesses the letter.

Oracy Skill: Ground Rules for Working Together

Hi, I'm Jack.

1 1.11 **Listen, look, and repeat.**

Ground Rules

1 Listen to others.

2 Take turns.

3 Respect others.

4 Share your ideas.

5 Raise your hand to speak.

Hi, I'm Liam.

Hi, I'm Kate.

Hi, I'm Emma.

2 **As a class, think of two more ground rules for working together.**

Let's Practice Oracy!

1. Form groups. Do the **Oracy Time!** task.
2. Remember to follow the ground rules.
3. Present your poster to the class.

Oracy Time!

Make a Color Poster

a As a group, decide on one color.

b Cut out or draw pictures for your color.

c Work together. Glue the pictures onto your poster.

This is our poster.
Our color is blue.

Check Your Oracy!

1 I listened to others.	**Yes / No**
2 I took turns.	**Yes / No**
3 I shared my ideas.	**Yes / No**

Learn to Write: Capital and Lowercase Letters

This is a capital letter: **E** This is a lowercase letter: **e**

1 Look and classify the letters.

CAPITAL LETTERS	W																		
lowercase letters	e	l	c	o	m	e													

2 Trace the capital letters in blue and the lowercase letters in red.

I'm Ted.

I'm from Turkey.

Time to Talk!

Game: Microphone

1 Stand in a circle.
2 Listen to some music as you pass around the microphone.
3 When the music stops, say the first letter of your name and country.
A (Azra). T (Turkey).

3 Write the first letter of your name in capitals.

______

AB pages 9–10

Unit 1B Ready to Read: Fiction

1 1.12 Key Words 4 Listen, point, and repeat.

old

slow

fast

tired

young

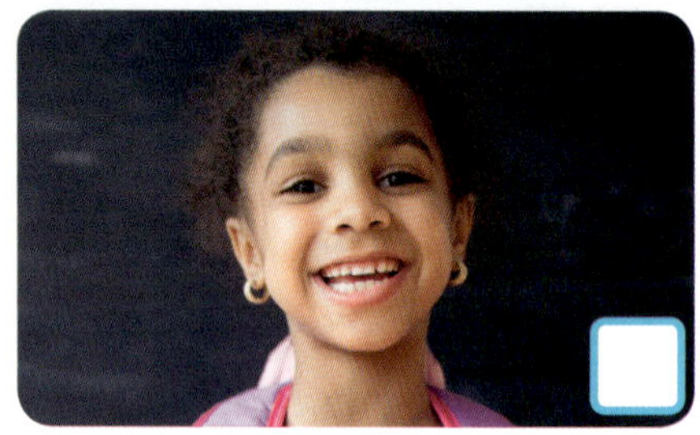
happy

2 1.13 Listen and number the pictures.

3 Draw something slow and something fast.

? Which words describe you?
I'm young.

old young fast slow happy

Reading Strategy: Real or Fantasy?

Stories can be: **real**  or **fantasy**. 

1 Look and circle the real things in green and the fantasy things in blue.

a 

b 

c 

d 

e 

f 

g 

2 Look and draw a real animal and a fantasy animal.

real

fantasy

Time to Talk!

What is your favorite story?

My favorite story is *Cinderella*.

Is it real or fantasy?

1.14

Grandma Turtle

by Andrea González

Grandma Turtle is very old. She is very, very old. She is 200 years old!

Grandma Turtle has a big shell. She has many wrinkles.

Think

How old is your grandma or grandpa?

Grandma Turtle loves to surf. But she is old, so she is very slow.

Grandma Turtle surfs alone. Young turtles aren't slow, they are too fast!

At night, Grandma Turtle is tired, very tired. She rests alone on the beach.

Think

When are you tired?

1.15 **Grandma Turtle**

One day, Grandma Turtle meets Young Turtle. He has a small shell. He is young, but he surfs slowly, too.

Grandma Turtle is surprised.

"You aren't old. You are young. Why do you surf slowly?" Grandma Turtle asks Young Turtle.

"I like it," says Young Turtle. "I am young, but I like to surf slowly."

Think

Is Young Turtle fast?

The sky is yellow, orange, purple, and blue.
Grandma Turtle and Young Turtle surf together.
They are happy.

Think

Are Grandma Turtle and Young Turtle different? Are they friends?

Explore the Text

1 1.16 Listen and match the pictures.

a 
young

b 
happy

c 
tired

d 
old

e 
slow

2 Number the pictures to tell the story.

3 Is the story *Grandma Turtle* real, or is it fantasy?

4 Number the opposites.

? Are you different from your friends?

Grammar: Verb *to be*: Affirmative and Negative

You are young. You aren't old. They are happy. They aren't slow.

1 Trace the words.

They are old.

You aren't twelve.

She is happy.

The ball isn't blue.

2 Trace and draw a picture.

You are young.

They are happy.

I am ______.

3 1.17 Listen and practice the rhyme.

I am special.
This is true.
<u>I am six.</u>
How about you?

They are special.
This is true.
<u>They are fast.</u>
How about you?

4 Say the rhyme using the underlined sentences in the negative.

Listening

1 1.18 **Listen, point, and repeat.**

1 
bicycle

2 
tablet

3 
colored pencils

4 
puzzle

5 
coloring book

6 
ball

2 1.19 **Listen and mark ✓ the objects that are mentioned.**

3 1.20 **Listen and number.**

1 

2 

3 

4 

old ☐
big ☐
small ☐
fast 1

Time to Talk!

Draw your favorite thing. Ask your classmate: "What's your favorite thing?"

My favorite thing is my bicycle.

Values AB page 16

How can we talk about ourselves?

Your challenge is to talk about yourself to the class.

1. **Make** a collage. Write your name and decorate it. You can cut out pictures of things you like, bring in photos, draw your favorite things, draw a cake with candles showing your age, etc.

2. **Work** in pairs. Lie on the floor on a large sheet of paper. Your partner traces around you. Then, switch and trace around each other.

3. **Glue** the drawings and photos on your cut-out body.

4. **Talk** about yourself to the class. Show your collage and say your first and last name, age, eye and hair color, favorite color, and where you are from.

Follow the ground rules when your classmates talk. Complete Check Your Oracy! in the Activity Book.

Who am I?
Look back through the unit. Share your ideas.

AB pages 17–19

SPEAKING MISSION

You are lost! Say who you are.

Before Your Mission

1 1.21 **Listen, point, and repeat.**

yes

no

name

phone

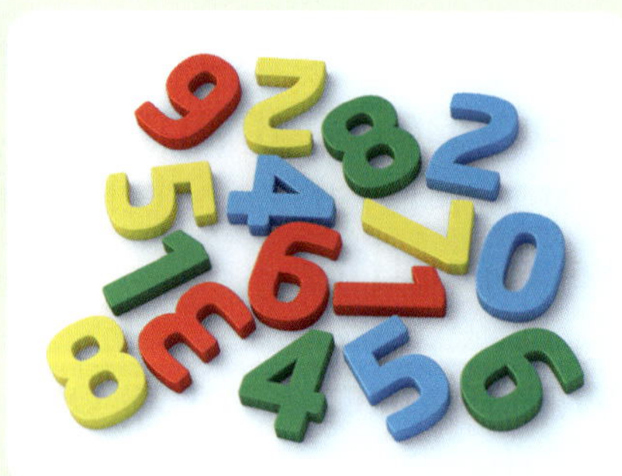
numbers

lost

2 1.22 **Listen and underline the correct answers.**

Name	Demir Kara	Demir Tosun
Age	6	5
Phone Number	3743-1235	3743-1238

Time to Talk!

Play the Telephone Game.

1 Tell your partner your phone number.
2 Your partner writes it down.

During Your Mission

3 1.23 **Listen and trace.**

What's your first name?	4268-9120.
What's your last name?	Sam.
How old are you?	Black.
What's your phone number?	I'm 6.

4 1.23 **Listen again. In pairs, role-play getting lost.**

Key Language

What's your first name?
What's your last name?
How old are you?
What's your phone number?

What makes you special?

2 What is school?

- Talk about school.
- Learn to agree or disagree.
- Use alphabetical order.
- Make a classroom map.
- Borrow school supplies.

Where are the children?

What school objects can you see?

What do you like about school?

2.1

Key Words 1

desk
teacher
classroom
gym
bathroom
playground

1 2.1 **Watch the video. Circle what is mentioned in the video.**

2 2.1 **Watch again. Complete the graphic organizer in the Activity Book.**

AB page 22

Unit 2A

Ready to Read: Nonfiction

Reading Strategy: Classifying

1 2.2 Listen, point, and repeat.

My Classroom

2 Cross out the one that doesn't belong in each group.

a

desks

chairs

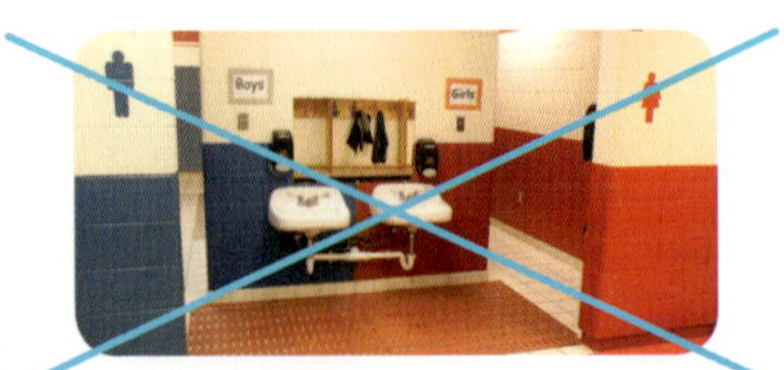
bathroom

b

gym

teacher

playground

c

teachers

classmates

windows

? What things are in your classroom? Chairs, desks, ...

2.3

Key Words 2

library

schoolbag

pencil case

notebook

colored pencil

eraser

2.4

Welcome to My School

I'm Tommy.
This is my school.
There is a gym,
a playground,
and a **library**.
I love my school!

This is my classroom. There are chairs, desks, and a board.
This is my teacher, Mr. Jones.
These are my classmates.
They're great!

Welcome to My School

This is my **schoolbag**. In my schoolbag, there is a **pencil case**, a **notebook**, and an apple. The apple is big and red. Yum!

In my pencil case, there are **colored pencils**, an **eraser**, and a ruler.

Think

Is there a gym in your school? Is there a library?

1 Classify. Draw lines from the words to the photos.

a school

b classroom

c schoolbag

gym desk bathroom colored pencils chair eraser

2 Draw other objects in the boxes.

My Classroom

My Schoolbag

3 2.6 Key Words 3 Listen and circle the correct picture.

1

2

What is your favorite place at school?
The playground.

Remember to listen to others.

Grammar: *a / an*

 **a** pencil

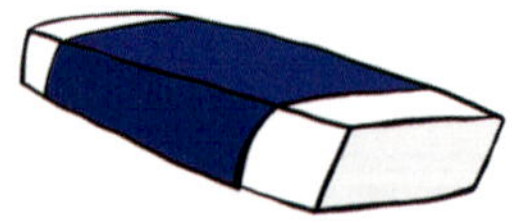 **an** eraser

1 🎧 2.7 Listen, repeat, and circle *a* or *an*.

1 a / an

2 a / an

3 a / an

4 a / an

5 a / an

6 a / an

2 Trace the words and draw the items in the schoolbag.

an apple

an eraser

a book

a pencil sharpener

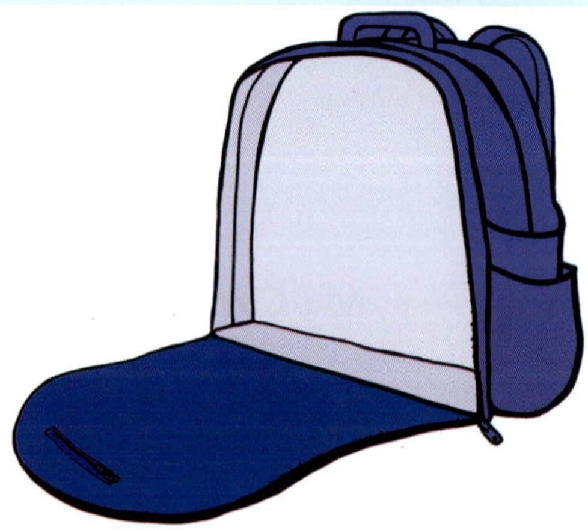

3 🎧 2.8 Listen and say the chant.

Dad! My schoolbag!
An apple, a pencil.
My book? Oh, look!
An eraser.
And my paper?

Time to Talk!

What's in your schoolbag?
An eraser, a ruler, and a book.

1 2.9 Listen, point, and repeat.

car

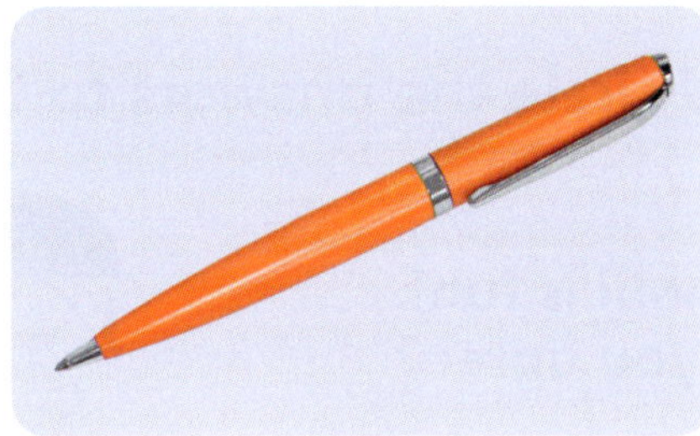

pen

ten

net

boy

hi

2 2.10 Listen and circle the picture with the same beginning sound.

1

c

2

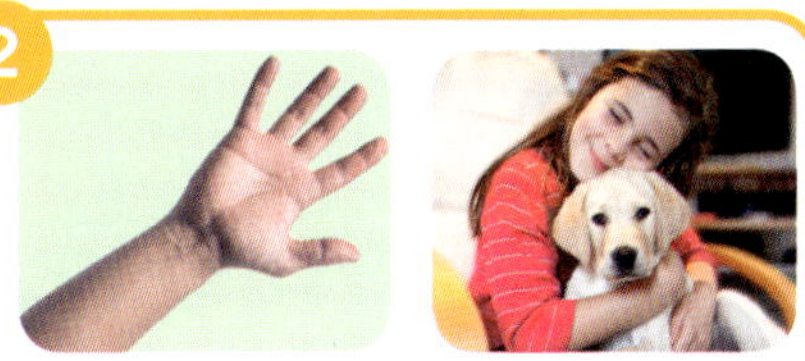

p

3

t

4

n

5

b

6

h

3 Say the word and underline the correct beginning sound.

c

b

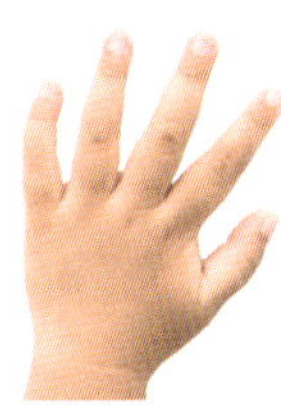

h

p

b

t

4 Form small groups. Look back at Unit 1 and find words beginning with *t* and *h*.

Oracy Skill: Agreeing and Disagreeing

1 ▶ 2.2 🎧 2.11 **Watch and circle the answers to the questions.**

a

School is fun! Do you agree?

Yes!

No!

b

Puzzles are fun! Do you agree?

Yes!

No!

Let's Practice Oracy! 2, 3

1 Listen to your teacher's opinion.

2 Say "Yes" if you agree or "No" if you disagree.

1

2

3

4

Check Your Oracy!

1 I participated.	Yes / No
2 I agreed and I disagreed.	Yes / No
3 I listened to my classmates.	Yes / No

Learn to Write: Alphabetical Order

1 2.12 Listen and say the alphabet.

A B C D E F G
H I J K L M N
O P Q R S T
U V W X Y Z

2 Write your name in your notebook and spell it out loud.

3 Look and write the words next to the correct beginning letters.

girl boy her cat

a	ant	**d**	desk	**g**	___ ___ ___ ___
b	___ ___ ___	**e**	eight	**h**	___ ___ ___
c	___ ___ ___	**f**	fish	**i**	iguana

Time to Talk!

What's the next letter?

1 Stand in a circle.

2 Take turns saying the letters in alphabetical order.

AB pages 29–30

Ready to Read: Fiction

1 2.13 **Key Words 4** Listen, point, and repeat.

story

sad

mad

hungry

lunchbox

surprised

2 2.14 Listen and draw the school object inside the schoolbag.

Reading Strategy: Understanding a Character's Feelings

He is **sad**.

1 2.15 **Listen and repeat.**

 happy  sad  surprised  mad

2 **How do these children feel?**

a 

b 

c 

d 

How do you feel at school?
I feel happy.

2.16

I Can't Find My Things!

by Silvia Zapiain

"Good morning, children," says Miss Brown.

"This is Max. It's his first day at school."

"Max, this is your desk," says Miss Brown.

Max sits down. He is happy.

Think

Why do you think Max is happy?

"Let's read a story!" says Miss Brown.

"Max, what's wrong?" asks Miss Brown.
"I'm sad. I can't find my book!"
"That's OK. You can read with Gemma."

Think
Who helps Max?

2.17 I Can't Find My Things!

"Let's draw a picture!" says Miss Brown.

"Max, what's wrong?" asks Miss Brown.

"I'm mad. I can't find my colored pencils!"

Gemma shares her pencils with Max.

"Lunchtime!" shout the children.

"Max, what's wrong now?" asks Miss Brown.

"I'm hungry. I can't find my lunchbox!"

Think

Why is Max mad? Why is he hungry?

Miss Brown is surprised.

"Max, show me your schoolbag, please," says Miss Brown.

"Oh, dear! Look out the window! Your book, your pencils, and your lunchbox are all on the playground!"

Think

Why are Max's things on the playground?

Explore the Text

1 Look at the story. Number the pictures in order.

2 Mark ✓ the things that Max can't find.

book

notebook

colored pencils

lunchbox

ruler

3 How do they feel? Circle the correct answers.

a 

Max is **mad** / **sad**.

c 

The teacher is **happy** / **surprised**.

b 

Max is **mad** / **hungry**.

d 

Max is **sad** / **mad**.

What makes you happy about school?
English class!

Grammar: Possessive Adjectives

This is **your** desk.
I can't find **my** book.
It is **his** first day at school.
Gemma shares **her** pencils with Max.

1 (2.18) Listen and match the sentences to the pictures.

a

b

1 This is **my** schoolbag.
2 This is **her** book.
3 This is **your** chair.
4 This is **his** schoolbag.

d

c

2 Trace the correct answers.

This is your / his present.

This is her / my dog.

Time to Talk!

Each student puts one school object in a bag. Take one object out of the bag and guess who it belongs to.
This is her pencil.

1 2.19 **Listen, point, and repeat.**

read books

play games

play sports

study

2 2.20 **What do you do in these places? Listen and match.**

a

b

study

play sports

read books

play games

c

d

3 2.20 **Listen again and sing the song.**

Agreeing and Disagreeing

1 Listen to your teacher give opinions about different activities.

2 Say "Yes" if you agree or "No" if you disagree.

3 Complete **Check Your Oracy!** on Activity Book page 37.

Oracy Time!

Reading is fun! Do you agree?

Yes. / No.

Playing sports is great!

Values AB page 36

How can we make a classroom map?

Your challenge is to present a classroom map to the class.

1. **Brainstorm** in small groups. Name all the things you can find in your classroom.
2. **Work** together to draw the shape of the classroom on a large sheet of paper.
3. **Cut out** colored paper shapes to represent different objects.
4. **Make** a key. See the example in the picture.
5. **Glue** the shapes on the map.
6. **Display** your classroom map on the wall.
7. **Present** your classroom map to other groups.

These are the books.

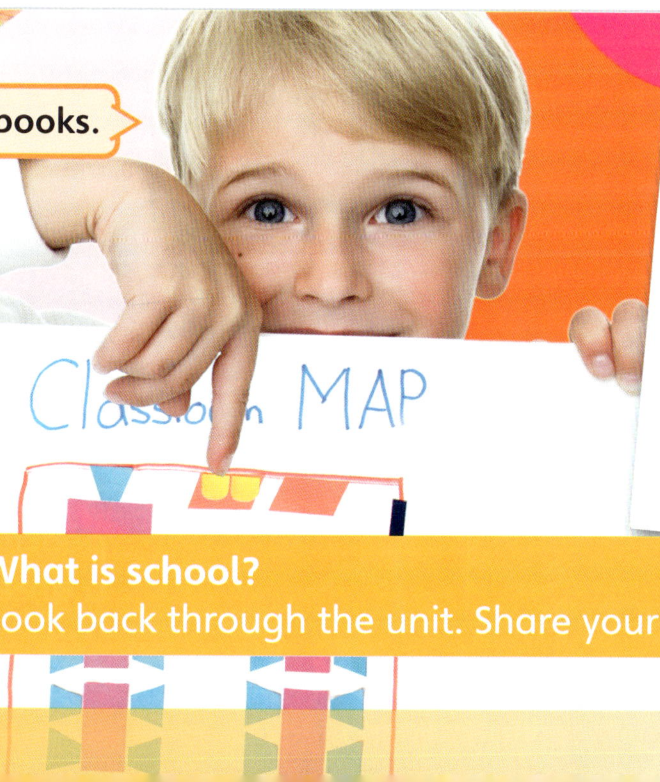

What is school?
Look back through the unit. Share your ideas.

AB pages 37–39

SPEAKING MISSION

You need to borrow something at school.

Before Your Mission

1 2.21 Listen and number the pictures.

scissors

1

crayon

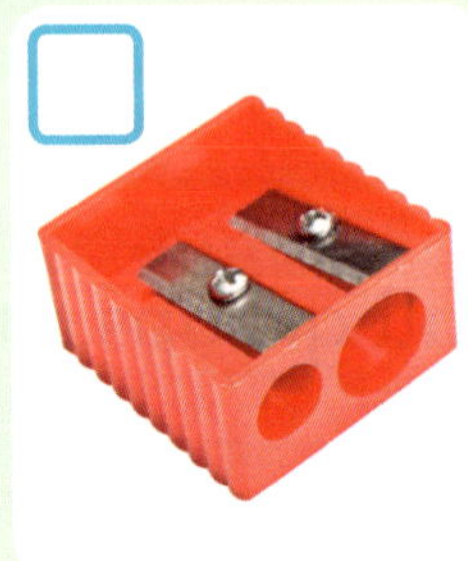
pencil sharpener

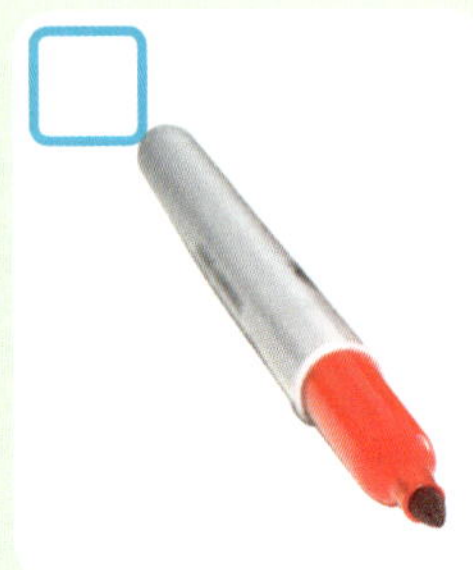
marker

ruler

glue

2 Circle the things you use in class.

3 Play Identify the Object.

One, red.

A pencil!

 Time to Talk!

Open your pencil case. Say what you have.

I have a red pencil. I have a green eraser.

During Your Mission

4 2.22 **Listen and mark ✓ the correct scenes.**

1

2

5 2.22 **Listen again and role-play the conversations in pairs.**

Key Language

Can I borrow your eraser?
Sure. Here you are.
Thank you.
Sorry! I don't have one.
No problem.

6 **Play the School Object Game in pairs.**

1 Choose three school objects.
2 Put the objects in your schoolbag.
3 Ask your partner for an object. If you guess what's in your partner's bag, you can borrow it!

3

What is a toy?

- ☐ **Talk** about toys.
- ☐ **Learn** how to listen to others.
- ☐ **Write** a complete sentence.
- ☐ **Make** a toy from recycled material.
- ☐ **Go** shopping for a toy.

What **toys** can you **see?**

What **colors** are they?

Are all toys **fun?**

3.1

Key Words 1

toy
box
house
paper
airplane
tablet

AB page 42

1. 3.1 **Watch the video. Circle the toys from the video.**

2. 3.1 **Watch again. Complete the graphic organizer in the Activity Book.**

Unit 3A

Ready to Read: Nonfiction

Reading Strategy: Classifying Words

1 3.2 **Listen and follow along.**

This is **Tim**.
He has a **car**.
The car is **blue**.

Tim

car

blue

2 **Match the words.**

1 name	a car
2 toy	b blue
3 color	c Tim

What colors are your toys?

3.3

Key Words 2

robot

fun

dollhouse

tent

train

jump rope

3.4

TOP FIVE TOYS

What are toys? Dolls, cars, or balls? Well, toys are many things. Read about the children's favorite toys!

This is Lucas.

He has a **robot**.

The robot says, "Stop! March! Sit! Stand!"

It's **fun**!

This is Olivia.

She has a **dollhouse**.

The dollhouse is white and blue.

3.5

TOP FIVE TOYS

This is Adrian.
He has a **tent**.
The tent is white with zigzags.

This is Emma.
She has a **jump rope**.
The jump rope is red.
It's fun to jump!

This is Angie.
She has a **train**.
The train is red, black, and green.

Think
Which is your favorite toy from the text?

1 Color the correct answer.

a Lucas has a robot / car.

b Olivia has a train / dollhouse.

c Adrian has a tent / tablet.

d Emma has a jump rope / robot.

e Angie has a train / tablet.

2 Color the word that doesn't belong in each list.

Name Words

Angie tent

Adrian

Toy Words

robot dollhouse

Olivia

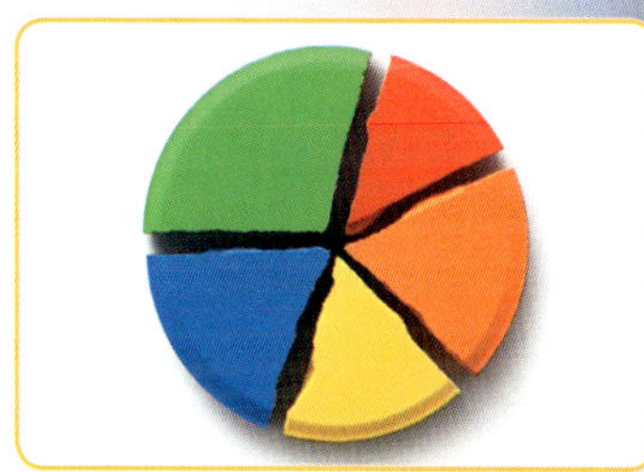

Color Words

train red

green

3 3.6 Key Words 3 Circle *children* and *jump* in the text. Label the pictures.

a

____

b

____

Imagine you're a toy. Which toy are you? I'm a/an ...

Grammar in Context

Grammar: Commands

Listen! March! Stop! Stand! Sit! Jump!

1 3.7 Listen to the robot. Number the commands in order.

Listen!

Stop!

Stand!

March!

Sit!

Jump!

2 3.8 Listen and follow the commands.

3 Form small groups.
Take turns giving commands.

Time to Talk!

What is your favorite toy?

My dinosaur.

Phonics

1 3.9 Listen, point, and repeat.

bat

cat

hat

pen

hen

ten

2 3.10 Listen and circle the correct word.

1

cat bat

2

pen hen

3

bat hat

3 Play in pairs. Point to a word. Your partner says the word.

cat	pen	hat
hen	bat	ten

Oracy Skill: Active Listening

1 3.2 3.11 **Watch the video. Circle the class that is listening.**

Class 1

Class 2

2 **Mark ✓ the pictures that show active listening.**

Let's Practice Oracy! 4

1. The teacher will name and do some actions. Repeat after him/her and follow.
2. 3.12 Listen to the song and do the actions.

Check Your Oracy!

1 Did you listen to your teacher?	**Yes / No**
2 Did you say "Please repeat that"?	**Yes / No**

Ready to Write

Learn to Write: Complete Sentences

A sentence gives a complete idea.

The ball is blue.

Paul has a slide.

This is a sentence:
She has a jump rope.

This is not a sentence:
a jump rope

1 Read and mark ✓ the sentences.

- [ ] my yo-yo
- [ ] I have a toy.
- [ ] red car
- [ ] I love my doll.

2 Read and trace. Then, draw a picture for the sentence.

I have a red car.

Time to Talk!

Class Competition

Make teams.
You have two minutes.

1 Say as many colors as you can.
2 Say as many toys as you can.

AB pages 49–50

Unit 3B Ready to Read: Fiction

1 3.13 Key Words 4 **Listen, point, and repeat.**

monkey bars

bike

car

action figure

dinosaur

spaceship

2 3.14 **Look, listen, and number the pictures.**

Time to Talk!

Look at the pictures. Tell a partner what you like and what you don't like.

I like the bike. I don't like the monkey bars.

Reading Strategy: Ordering Story Events

1 3.15 **Listen and number the story events in order.**

2 3.15 **Listen again and number the sentences.**

- [ ] Thank you, mom.
- [1] I'm hungry.
- [ ] I'm sad.
- [ ] I'm so happy!

What toys do you and your friends play with at school?
We play with …

Don't Touch!

By Irma Calvo

Hiro and Olivia
are friends.
They are at the park.

They play on the monkey bars.
They play on the swings. They ride
their bikes. They have lots of fun.

Then, they sit on the grass. They open their backpacks. The backpacks are full of toys.

There's a problem. Hiro and Olivia don't want to share their toys.

"Don't touch my cars!" says Hiro. "They're mine!"

"Don't touch my action figures!" says Olivia. "They're mine!"

"And don't touch my dinosaur," says Hiro.

"And don't touch my spaceship," says Olivia.

Think

Your friend says, "Don't touch my toys!" Does it make you feel happy or sad?

3.17 Don't Touch!

The children are mad. They sit quietly. They play alone. They get bored.

Hiro looks at Olivia. "Do you want to play with me?"

"Can I play with your cars?" asks Olivia.

"OK," says Hiro. "Can I play with your spaceship?"

"OK," says Olivia.

Think

Why do Olivia and Hiro get bored?

The friends play together.
They have lots of fun.

"Let's play again tomorrow," says Olivia.
"Yes!" says Hiro.

Think

What do you share with your friends?

Explore the Text

1 Look at the story. Number the pictures in order.

2 Look at Activity 1 and number the sentences in order.

- [ ] They play on the swings.
- [ ] They play together. They have lots of fun.
- [ ] "Don't touch my action figures!"
- [1] Olivia and Hiro are at the park.
- [ ] "Can I play with your spaceship?"
- [ ] "Let's play again tomorrow."

Do you like to share your toys? Why or why not?

Grammar: Negative Command

Don't touch my cars!

Don't run!

1 3.18 Listen and number. Then, listen again, point, and repeat.

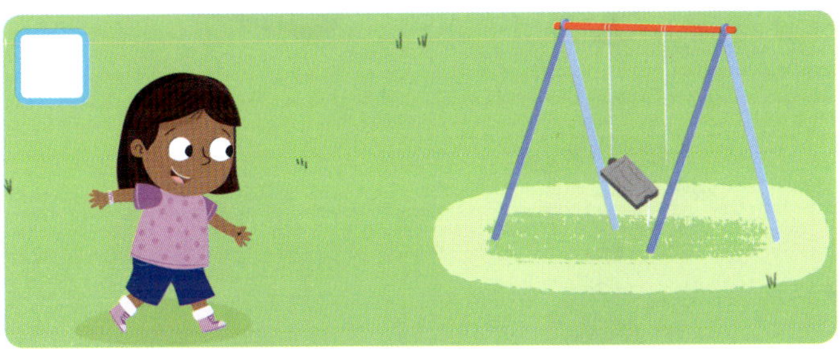

2 Look at the pictures and give commands.

spider

plant

scissors

Don't touch the ...

3 Play a game with a partner.

You and your partner are robots.
Give your partner commands.

Don't run!

Sit down!

Listening

1 3.19 **Listen and circle.**

a The children are playing a game.
b The children are reading a book.

2 3.19 **Listen again and circle the two toys.**

3 **Play the game with a partner.**

Active Listening

1 Choose a toy.
2 Walk around. Ask the **Oracy Time!** question about the toy.
3 Listen actively and answer the questions.
4 Complete **Check Your Oracy!** in the Activity Book on page 57.

Oracy Time!

Do you like (action figures)?
Yes. / No.
Please repeat that.

Values AB page 56

How can we make a toy?

Your challenge is to make a toy with recycled materials.

1. **Work** in small groups. Talk about your favorite toys.
2. **Bring** clean recycled materials to class.
3. **Work** together to make a toy.
4. **Present** your toy to the class.
5. **Play** with all the toys you made.

What is a toy?
Look back through the unit. Share your ideas.

AB pages 57–59

1 Look and match.

Listening to others | Agreeing and disagreeing | Ground rules

YOUR TASK

a In pairs, choose three toys on page 71. Agree or disagree with your partner.

Let's buy a jump rope. Do you agree?

Yes.

b 3.20 Listen and circle the correct toy on page 71.

A ball, please.

Here you go.

Thank you.

c Play Store with your partner. Remember your ground rules.

yo-yo

play dough

boat

board game

bike

action figure

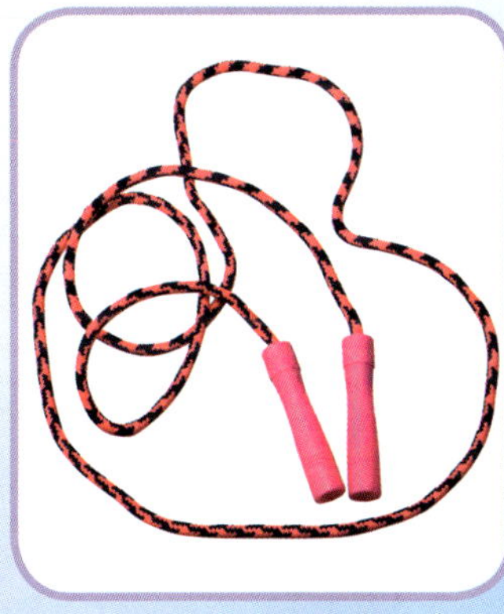
jump rope

soccer ball

doll

dinosaur

jigsaw puzzle

dollhouse

Check Your Oracy!

	☺	☺☺	☺☺☺
1 I listened.			
2 I agreed and disagreed.			
3 I took turns.			

4 What makes a home?

- ☐ **Talk** about home.
- ☐ **Learn** how to take turns.
- ☐ **Identify** nouns.
- ☐ **Describe** your home.
- ☐ **Find** your toys.

What can you see?

Do people live in these homes?

Which home is your favorite?

4.1

Key Words 1

home
family
dining room
living room
bedroom
kitchen

1 4.1 **Watch the video. Circle the actions from the video.**

cook

read

swim

watch TV

2 4.1 **Watch again. Complete the graphic organizer in the Activity Book.**

AB page 62

Ready to Read: Nonfiction

Reading Strategy: Comparing

1 4.2 Listen, point, and repeat.

2 4.3 Listen and circle the correct answers.

Ahmet

a

b

BIG SMALL

c

Sabita

a

b

BIG SMALL

c

Compare your bedroom to Ahmet's and Sabita's bedrooms.
Ahmet's bedroom is big. My bedroom is small.

4.4

Key Words 2

apartment

room

water

garden

stove

bed

4.5

All Kinds of Homes

What is a home?
There are all kinds of homes!

This is Lisa's home. It's an **apartment**. It's big! It has seven **rooms**—a bathroom, a kitchen, a living room, a dining room, and three bedrooms.

Her favorite place is her bedroom.

Look! It's Lisa's cat. Where is it? It's in the kitchen.

4.6

All Kinds of Homes

This is Akila's home. It's a houseboat. It floats on **water**. It has a kitchen, a living room, a bathroom, and two bedrooms.

Look! It has a **garden**, too. Where is it? It's on the roof.

This is Pablo's home. It's a tree house. You climb stairs to get inside. It has four rooms—a kitchen, a living room, and two bedrooms.

Where's the bathroom? It's under the tree house.

This is Kallic's home. It's an igloo. It has one big room. It has a **stove** and a big **bed**.

Think

Which house is your favorite?

1 4.5 4.6 Listen again. Circle the number of rooms and draw.

Lisa	Rooms	Apartment
	1 2 3 4 5 6 7	
Akila	**Rooms**	**Houseboat**
	1 2 3 4 5 6 7	
Pablo	**Rooms**	**Tree House**
	1 2 3 4 5 6 7	
Kallic	**Rooms**	**Igloo**
	1 2 3 4 5 6 7	

2 4.7 Key Words 3 Listen and repeat. Circle the words *roof* and *stairs* in the nonfiction text. Label the pictures.

1

2

3 Draw your home in your notebook and tell your classmates about it.

This is my house. It's orange and white.

What's special about your home?
It has a garden.

Grammar: Prepositions

Where's Lisa's cat?	It's **in** the kitchen.
Where's Akila's garden?	It's **on** the roof.
Where's the bathroom?	It's **under** the tree house.

1 Where's the cat? Color the correct option.

a on in under

b on in under

c on in under

2 4.8 Listen and number the pictures.

a

b

Time to Talk!

1 Draw your bedroom.
Include your bed, favorite toy, a schoolbag, and a pet.

2 Ask questions in pairs.

Where is your toy?

It's on my bed.

1 4.9 Listen, point, and repeat.

nut

cut

hut

big

wig

dig

2 4.10 Listen and underline the correct words.

a

cut hut

b

wig big

c

but nut

d

big fig

3 4.11 Listen and sing the songs.

Look at this chick.
His name is Stig.
He has a wig,
A big, big wig!
He likes to dig,
With his big wig.
His name is Stig.

Nuts, nuts,
I love nuts.
A nut in a hut.
Big nuts,
Peanuts,
Any kind of nut.
I love nuts!

Oracy Skill: Taking Turns

1 4.2 4.12 **Watch and answer the questions.**

a Are they playing a game or doing their homework?
b What does Jack say at the end?
c Are they taking turns?

Let's Practice Oracy! 5, 6

1 Form pairs. Play Tic-Tac-Toe.

2 Remember to take turns.

Check Your Oracy!

1 I played.	Yes / No
2 I took turns.	Yes / No
3 I spoke in English.	Yes / No

Learn to Write: Nouns

A noun is a place, a person, an animal, or an object.

place

person

animal

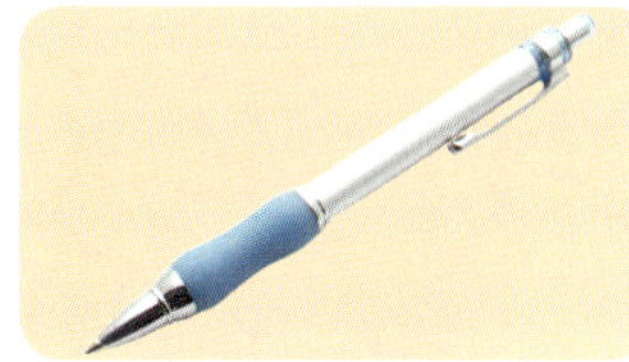
object

1 Look and number the pictures.

1 Place   2 Person   3 Animal   4 Object

boy [2]

turtle [ ]

bathroom [ ]

teacher [ ]

ball [ ]

gym [ ]

hen [ ]

book [ ]

2 Draw a place, a person, an animal, and an object.

Time to Talk!

Game: What Is It?

1 Form two teams.

2 Your teacher will show you some photos. Say if the photo is a place, person, animal, or object.

Remember to take turns.

AB pages 69–70

Unit 4B

Ready to Read: Fiction

1 4.13 Key Words 4 **Listen, point, and repeat.**

snail

ladybug

forest

spider

butterfly

mouse

2 **Match the animals with their homes.**

a

b

c

1

2

3

3 **In your notebook, draw an animal inside its home.**

Do you have a pet at home?

Reading Strategy: Plot and Setting

Plot: What is the story about?

A girl and two lambs.

Setting: Where does the story take place?

On a farm.

1 **Look at the book cover. Circle the correct answer.**

a Plot: What is the story about?

Friends. **Homes.**

b Setting: Where does the story take place?

On the beach. **In the forest.**

Time to Talk!

Think of your favorite story.
What is it about?
Where does it take place?

4.14

Snail Finds His Home

by Silvia Zapiain

"My home! My home!" says Snail sadly.

"What's the matter?" asks Ladybug.

"I can't find my home!"

"Let's go and find it!"

So, off they go into the forest.

Think

Why is Snail sad?

They see Spider.

"Hey! What's the matter?" asks Spider.

"I can't find my home," says Snail.

"Let's go and find it!"

They see Butterfly.

"What's the matter?" asks Butterfly.

"I can't find my home," says Snail.

"Is it under a leaf?" asks Butterfly.

"No, it isn't," says Snail.

Think

Are Snail, Ladybug, Spider, and Butterfly friends?

4.15 Snail Finds His Home

They see Mouse.

"Hey! What's the matter?" asks Mouse.

"I can't find my home," says Snail.

"Let's go and find it!"

Suddenly, there is a loud noise.

"What's that?" asks Mouse.

"It's a storm!" says Ladybug. "Let's find a place to hide from the rain!"

Think

What makes a loud noise in a storm?

Where is Butterfly? She's under the tree on a rock.

Where is Mouse? Is he under a tree?

No, he isn't. He's in a hole.

And Ladybug? She's under a leaf.

Is Spider under the leaf, too? Yes, he is.

"Eek!" says Snail. It starts to rain. He goes inside his shell.

"It's really warm in here," says Snail.

"This is my home!"

Think

Do you think Snail is happy now? Why?

Explore the Text

1 **Circle the answers.**

a Plot: What is the story about?

Snail and Butterfly.

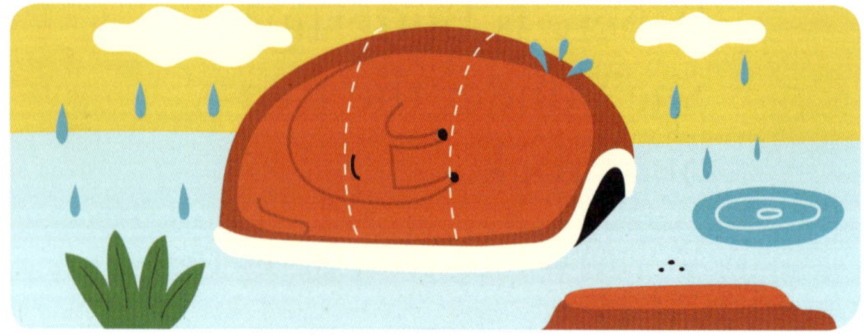

Snail finds a home.

b Setting: Where does the story take place?

In the park.

In the forest.

2 **Color the answers.**

a

Ladybug is under / in / on Snail's shell.

b

The friends are under / in / on the tree.

c

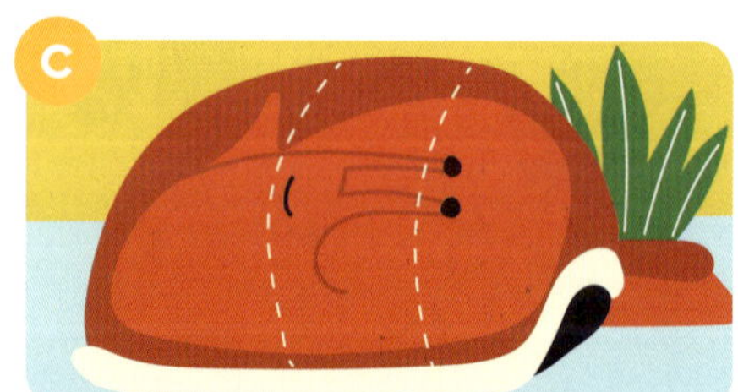

Snail is under / in / on his shell.

3 **Number the pictures and retell the story.**

Grammar: Verb *to be*: *Yes/No* Questions

Is Mouse under a tree?
No, he isn't. He's in a hole.

Is Spider under the leaf?
Yes, he is.

1 4.16 **Where is the red marker? Listen and circle the correct answer.**

2 **Match the questions to the correct answers and trace.**

1 Is the mouse on the chair?
2 Is the mouse under the chair?

a No, it isn't.
b Yes, it is.

Time to Talk!

1 Two classmates leave the classroom.
2 Hide a small ball somewhere in the classroom.
3 The two classmates come back in and guess where the ball is.

Is it under the teacher's desk?
No, it isn't.

Listening

1 4.17 **Listen to the poem. Circle the correct answer.**

What is the poem about?

A person. **An animal.** **A place.** **An object.**

2 4.17 **Listen again. Point to the actions in the order you hear them.**

I eat.

I draw.

I sleep.

I get love.

I paint.

I read.

I am myself.

I play.

Taking Turns

1 Draw what home means to you in the frame.

2 In groups, take turns showing your drawing. Remember to say, "It's your turn."

3 Complete **Check Your Oracy!** on Activity Book page 77.

Home is …

Values AB page 76

How can I describe my home?

Your challenge is to show and describe your home to the class.

1. **Use** construction paper to make a big envelope.
2. **Draw** your home on it.
3. **Draw** six separate pictures about your home. For example, you can draw pictures of your family, a pet, your bedroom, or your favorite toys.
4. **Put** the drawings inside the envelope.
5. **Show** your home to the class. Take out your drawings one at a time and describe your home.

This is my home. My home is my family.

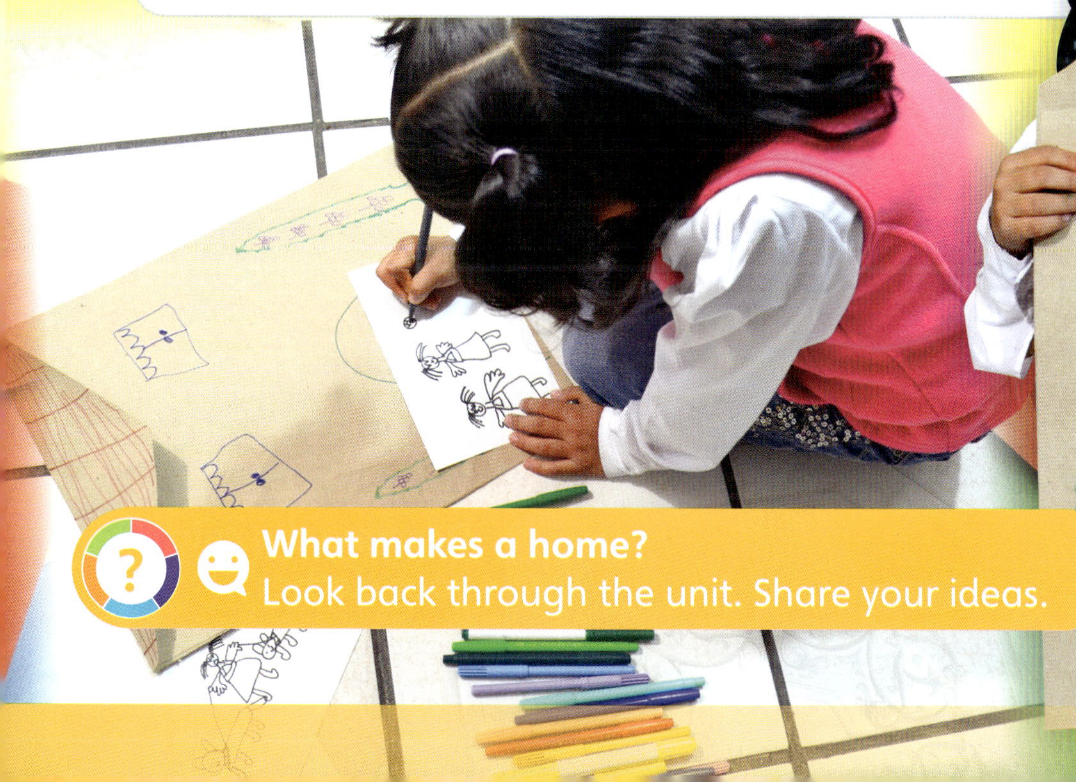

What makes a home?
Look back through the unit. Share your ideas.

AB pages 77–79

SPEAKING MISSION

You lost an object and you need to find it.

Before Your Mission

1 4.18 **Listen, point, and repeat.**

socks

T-shirt

hat

jacket

skirt

glasses

2 4.19 **Listen and play the Pointing Game with the pictures above.**

Time to Talk!

Describe the color of your clothes.

During Your Mission

3 4.20 **Listen and mark ✓ where the jacket is.**

4 **What is something you always lose? Draw a picture and cut it out.**

Key Language

Where is my English book?

I can't find it!

Where is it?

Is it in the schoolbag?

Is it on the shelf?

Is it under the chair?

Yes, it is.

No, it isn't.

5 **Play in pairs. Hide your picture *in*, *on*, or *under* something. Your partner tries to guess where it is.**

? Is your bedroom neat? Do you lose your things there?

5 Where do wild animals belong?

- Talk about wild animals.
- Learn to participate actively.
- Identify questions and exclamations.
- Make animal masks.
- Play a board game.

Where do these animals live?

What are their favorite foods?

Which one is your favorite?

5.1

Key Words 1

zebra
land
elephant
octopus
ocean
dolphin

1 5.1 **Watch the video. Number the animals in the order they appear.**

elephant

zebra

dolphin

octopus

2 5.1 **Watch again. Complete the graphic organizer in the Activity Book.**

AB page 82

Unit 5A

Ready to Read: Nonfiction

Reading Strategy: Visualizing

1 5.2 Listen, point, and repeat.

crocodile

parrot

penguin

blue whale

brown bear

panda

2 5.3 Listen to three animal sounds. Guess the animals.

3 5.4 Listen and visualize the animal. What is it?

4 5.5 Listen, visualize the animal, and draw it.

Which animals in the pictures are wild?

Remember to raise your hand to speak.

5.6

Key Words 2

5.7

Top Five Wild Animals

Look! These are my top five wild animals!

#5 Crocodile

Crocodiles live on land and in water. They have big **teeth** and a long **tail**. Their favorite foods are fish, frogs, and birds.

#4 Parrot

Parrots have **beaks** and feathers. Their favorite foods are fruit and insects.

They live in the **jungle**. What color are they?

They are blue, red, green, yellow, orange, and white!

5.8 Top Five **Wild** Animals

#3 Blue Whale

Blue whales live in the ocean. They're very, very, very big—as big as three school buses!

#2 Brown Bear

Brown bears live in the forest.

Their favorite foods are plants and small animals.

They have long claws.

#1 Panda

This is my number one wild animal, the giant panda! Giant pandas are bears, too! But their favorite food is bamboo. Pandas have black and white fur. They live in the forest.

Think

Which animals walk on four legs?

Explore the Text

5A

1 Match the animals to their homes.

a 
brown bear

c 
parrot

b 
blue whale

forest

ocean

jungle

2 5.7 5.8 Read and listen to the text again. Mark ✓ the correct answer.

a teeth		b fur	
 ✓	 ☐	 ☐	 ☐

3 5.9 Key Words 3 Listen and repeat.
Label the pictures *F* (feathers) or *I* (insects).

a 
____

b 
____

4 Visualize an imaginary animal made up of two wild animals. Draw it and name it.

panda + penguin = panguin

It's a panda and a penguin. It's a panguin!

? Where does your favorite wild animal live?

Grammar in Context

Grammar: Verb *to be*: *Wh–* Questions

What color are they? They are black and white.
What are they? They're baby pandas.

1 🎧 5.10 **Listen to the chant. Mark ✓ the correct picture.**

a 

b 

c 

2 🎧 5.10 **Listen again and match.**

1 What are they?
2 What color are they?
3 Where are they?

a They're red, yellow, green, white, and blue.
b They're in the zoo.
c They're parrots.

3 **Look and guess. What are they?**

What are they?

They're claws.

a 

b 

c 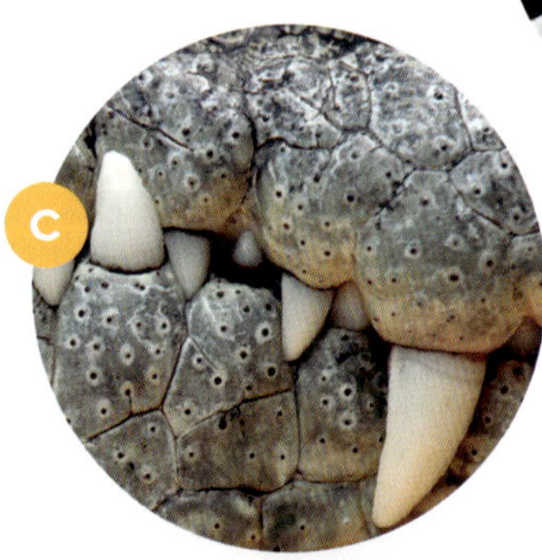

d 

e 

f 

Time to Talk!

Guess the Animals

Describe your favorite animal.

They have big feet. They're gray or brown. They live on land. What are they?

Elephants.

1 5.11 Listen, point, and repeat.

queen

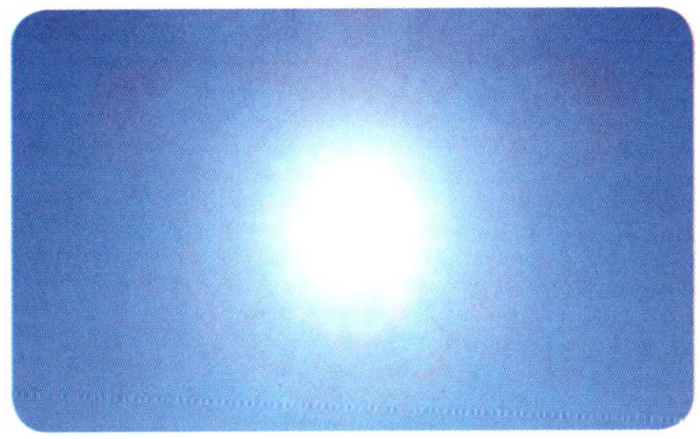

sun

fish

jar

goat

ring

2 5.12 Listen and say the chant.

Look! A queen, a queen, a queen,
Sitting in the sun, the sun, the sun.
She is having fun!

Look! A fish, a fish, a fish,
Swimming in a jar, a jar, a jar.
It can't swim very far!

Look! A goat, a goat, a goat,
With a golden ring, a ring, a ring.
See how it can sing!

3 5.13 Listen and complete the words with *q*, *s*, *f*, *j*, *g*, or *r*.

a I have a big white ____abbit.

b Please, close the ____ate.

c Let's sing a ____ong.

d The fish moves its ____ins.

e Sharks have big ____aws.

f This is a difficult ____uiz.

Oracy

Oracy Skill: Participating Actively

1 ▶ 5.2 🎧 5.14 **Watch and mark ✓ what they agree to do.**

draw pictures ☐

play with dolls ☐

play charades ☐

2 🎧 5.14 **Listen again. Circle the phrases you hear.**

Let's ...! | OK! | Please. | Yes!

Let's Practice Oracy!

1. Form pairs.
2. Look at the activities in **Oracy Time!**
3. Agree on an activity to do together.

Oracy Time!

ride bikes

play soccer

play with marbles

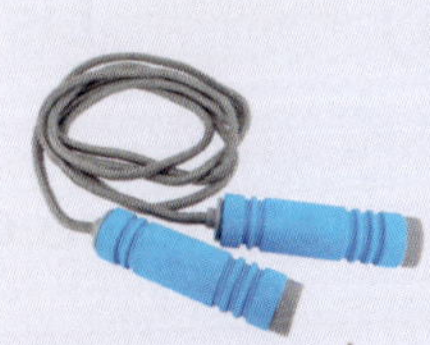

jump rope

Check Your Oracy!

1 I participated.	Yes / No
2 I used the cue card.	Yes / No
3 I listened to my partner.	Yes / No

Ready to Write

5A

Learn to Write: Identify Questions and Exclamations

What's your favorite animal? Happy Birthday!

1 **Point to the question marks (?) and exclamation points (!) in the photos. Write them in the boxes.**

a 

b 

c 

d 

e 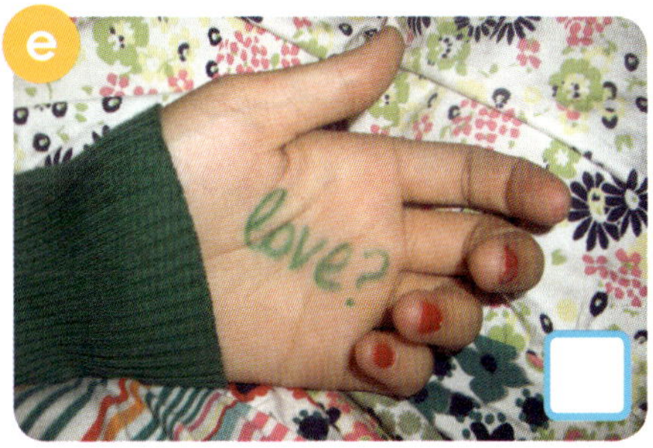

f 

2 5.15 **Listen and repeat.**

a Is it a parrot?
b Hello!
c Let's play!
d What color are they?

3 5.16 **Listen. Write ? for questions or ! for exclamations.**

a ? b ___ c ___ d ___

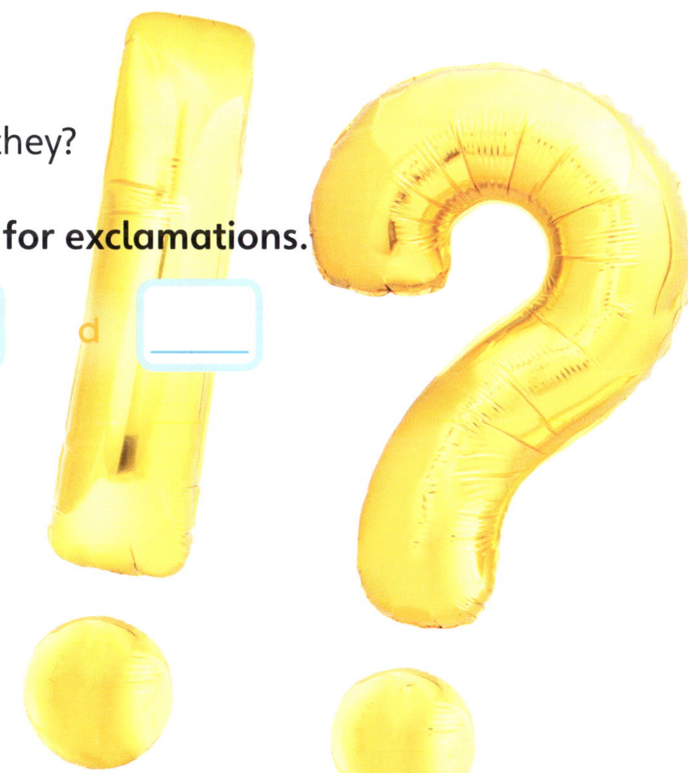

Time to Talk!

Don't Stop!

Sit in a circle. Take turns saying an exclamation or a question.

A: How old are you?
B: What's your name?
C: Come!

AB pages 89–90

Ready to Read: Fiction

1 5.17 Key Words 4 Listen, point, and repeat.

rabbit

moon

snake

tongue

sun

stars

2 5.18 Listen and number the pictures.

3 Draw suns  , stars  , flowers , and  hearts on the animals.

Time to Talk!

In pairs, give each other instructions.

Draw two hearts.

Remember to take turns.

Reading Strategy: Predicting from Pictures

1 Look at the picture. Which animal comes in next?

2 Look at the pictures. What comes next? Draw a picture.

a

→

b

→

5.19

The Rabbit on the Moon

by Andrea González

Ketzi is a snake. She is an artist. Her tongue is her paintbrush! Her tongue is green, yellow, and orange.

Look at her pictures! Yellow hearts on the frogs, green flowers on the birds, and orange suns on the fish.

One day, Ketzi is under a tree. A little rabbit is with her, too.

"I'm hungry!" says Ketzi.

"Here you are! Eat my carrot."

"No, thank you. My favorite food is white," Ketzi says.

"White food? Mmm … I'm white. Eat me!" the rabbit says.

"No! You're only a little rabbit, and you are so cute."

Think

What are rabbits' favorite foods?
What are snakes' favorite foods?

5.20 The Rabbit on the Moon

"Hug me, little rabbit! Let's fly!"

Are Ketzi and the little rabbit near the stars? Yes, they are!

They dance around the moon.

Think

Why do Ketzi and the rabbit dance?

Look! Ketzi is drawing on the moon!

That's a picture of the little rabbit!

Now, Ketzi and the little rabbit are friends forever.

Look at the full moon at night. A picture of the little rabbit is on the moon.

Think

Can you see a little rabbit on the moon?

Explore the Text

1 **Number the pictures in order. Retell the story with a partner.**

2 **Circle *T* (true) or *F* (false).**

a Ketzi is a snake. **T F**
b The rabbit is hungry. **T F**
c Ketzi's favorite food is yellow. **T F**
d Ketzi eats the rabbit. **T F**

3 **What comes next? Imagine and draw.**

? Which wild animals are not good friends?

Grammar: Verb *to be*: *Yes/No* Questions

Are Ketzi and the little rabbit near the stars? Yes, they are. / No, they aren't.

1 5.21 Listen and circle *Yes* or *No*.

a Yes / No b Yes / No c Yes / No d Yes / No

2 5.21 Listen again and answer *Yes, they are* or *No, they aren't*.

Are zebras black and white?

Yes, they are.

3 Look at the pictures and ask questions starting with *Are they ... ?*

Are they in the jungle?

No, they aren't. They're in the forest.

1 5.22 Listen, point, and repeat.

1 
nose

2 
eyes

3 
legs

4 
ears

5 
wings

6 
feet

2 Which animals can you see in the pictures? Guess.

It's a bear!

3 5.23 Listen and number the animals.

Participating Actively

1 Form groups.
2 Choose an animal to imitate.
3 Take turns imitating the animal.
4 Remember to participate actively using *Let's … !*
5 Complete **Check Your Oracy!** on Activity Book page 97.

Let's be butterflies!

Where do the animals in the pictures live?
The frog lives on land and in water.

Values AB page 96

How can we describe a wild animal?

Your challenge is to describe a wild animal.

1. **Choose** your favorite wild animal.
2. **Make** a mask of your wild animal.
3. **Think** of things to say about your animal: body parts, habitat, color, favorite food, etc.
4. **Present** your animal to the class.

Where do wild animals belong?
Look back through the unit and share your ideas.

AB pages 97–99

SPEAKING MISSION

Play a board game.

Before Your Mission

1 5.24 **Listen, point, and repeat.**

board game

dice

game piece

square

lose

win

2 **Look, read, and number.**

1 board game 2 square 3 game piece

Time to Talk!

Play Animal Charades.

Grrr …

Are you a tiger?

Yes, I am!

During Your Mission

3 5.25 **Listen. What are the girls doing?**

4 **Play the Animal Game.** One, two, three. It's a dolphin.

Key Language

You start.

Throw the dice.

It's my turn.

It's your turn.

I win!

? Where do the animals in the game belong?

6 What can people do?

- Talk about your abilities.
- Learn to agree or disagree.
- Identify an action verb.
- Make a spinner.
- Agree on what to play together.

What can the children do?

Can you do these things?

Can everyone do the same things?

6.1

Key Words 1

ability
paint
run
skate
play basketball
talk

1 ▶ 6.1 **Watch the video. Mark ✓ the actions you see.**

dance ☐

draw ☐

swim ☐

paint ☐

play basketball ☐

2 ▶ 6.1 **Watch again. Complete the graphic organizer in the Activity Book.**

AB page 102

Unit 6A Ready to Read: Nonfiction

Reading Strategy: Predicting from Titles

1 Match the story titles with the pictures.

1

3

2
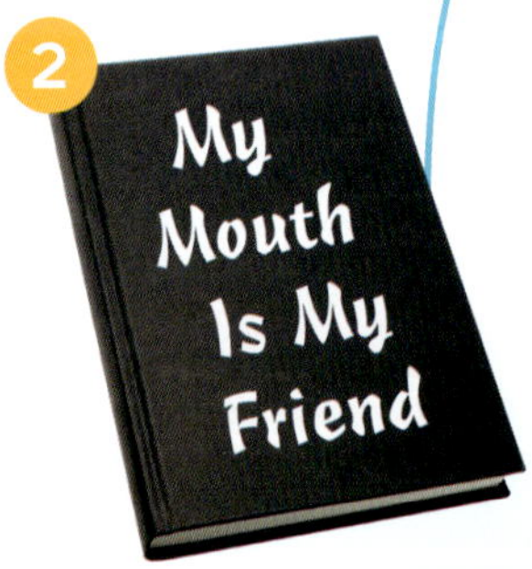

4

a

b

c

d

2 Read the title and draw two things the story may be about.

I Love My Home

Time to Talk!

Form pairs. Say the title of your favorite story. Ask your partner to draw two things the story may be about.

My favorite story is *The Little Prince*.

6.2

Key Words 2

see

ride

climb

say

spell

swim

6.3

Kids with Amazing Abilities

Hi! I'm Sven. I'm seven years old. I can clap 120 times in one minute.

My name is Ethan. I'm blind, which means I can't **see**. But I can **ride** a horse and **climb** trees!

6.4

Kids with *Amazing* Abilities

I'm Sharie. I can talk in a funny way. I can **say** and **spell** words backwards! Look! CAT is TAC, and BOOK is KOOB.

Can you do that?

My name's Buassi. I'm ten. I can **swim** in the ocean with my eyes open for a long time. I can see underwater like a dolphin!

Can you see like a dolphin underwater?

Hi, I'm Carl. I can't walk, but I can play basketball.

What are your special abilities?

Think

What makes Carl amazing?

1 6.3 6.4 **Read and listen to the text again. Circle the correct answers.**

Who says these things?

a "I can play basketball."

b "I can swim underwater like a dolphin."

c "I can't see."

d "I can say and spell words backwards."

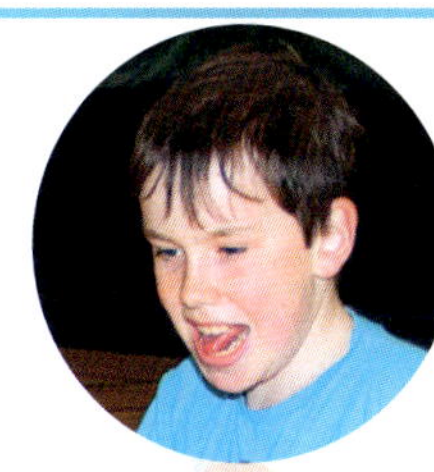

2 6.5 Key Words 3 **Listen and repeat. Circle the words *blind* and *backwards* in the nonfiction text. Label the pictures.**

a

____

b

____

3 **Choose one more picture for the text *Kids with Amazing Abilities*.**

How fast can you clap? Count your claps in one minute.

Grammar in Context

Grammar: ***I can … / I can't …***

I can ride a horse. **I can't walk.**

1 6.6 **Listen, look, and sing.**

I can , and I can .

I can , and I can .

I can , and I can ,

But …

I can't do everything!

I can't , and I can't .

I can't  well at night,

But …

I can do lots of things!

2 6.6 **Listen again. What can the boy do? Mark ✓ or ✗.**

run

write

read

swim

Time to Talk!

Tell your partner things you can and can't do.

I can read. I can't ride a bike.

1 6.7 Listen, point, and repeat.

hop

top

pop

mad

bad

dad

2 6.8 Listen and sing the song.

Do the hop dance!
Hop, hop,
Hop, hop, hop!
Get off your seat!
Dance to the beat!

Do the top dance!
Top, top,
Top, top, top!
Get off your seat!
Dance to the beat!

Do the pop dance!
Pop, pop,
Pop, pop, pop!
Get off your seat!
Dance to the beat!

3 6.9 Listen to the chant. Complete the words.

m__________ b__________ d__________

Oracy Skill: Asking for Agreement

1 6.2 6.10 **Watch and circle the phrases and words you hear.**

Can you play? | Do you agree?

Yes. | No.

2 6.10 **Listen again. Who says *Yes* and who says *No*? Write *Yes* or *No* in the speech bubbles.**

Let's Practice Oracy! 2, 3, 8

1. Form small groups.
2. Read the topics in **Oracy Time!** out loud. Ask your classmates if they agree or disagree.

Oracy Time!

Spelling is fun.
Swimming is difficult.
Tying your shoes is easy.
Fish is delicious.
Spiders are scary.

Check Your Oracy!

1 I listened to others.	**Yes / No**
2 I agreed or disagreed.	**Yes / No**
3 I respected my classmates' opinions.	**Yes / No**

Learn to Write: Verbs

A verb can tell about an action.

run

read

paint

1 Look and circle the verbs.

a

eat
sandwich

b

park
run

c

game
play

d

paint
picture

2 Underline the verbs and draw.

The boy reads a book.

The girl plays the piano.

Time to Talk!

Game: Act it Out!

1 Play in pairs.
2 Say a verb.
3 Your partner acts it out!

Remember to respect others.

AB pages 109–10

Unit 6B

Ready to Read: Fiction

1 6.11 Key Words 4 **Listen, point, and repeat.**

music

love

dancer

practice

read

puppy

2 **Read and underline what is true about you.**

a I **can** / **can't** play music.
b I **practice** / **don't practice** English at home.
c I **am** / **am not** a good dancer.
d I **can** / **can't** read in English.
e I **have** / **don't have** a puppy.
f I **like** / **don't like** hip-hop music.

Time to Talk!

Work in small groups.
Share your answers.
I can play music. I practice English at home.

Why can people do different things?

Reading Strategy: Cause and Effect

Cause → Effect

1 Look and match the cause with the effect.

Cause:

1 

2 

3 

4 

Effect:

a 

b 

c 

d 

2 Look at the cause and draw the effect.

→

When you can't do something, what do you do?

Hip-hop Hanna

6.12

by Irma Calvo

Hanna loves music. She loves dance movies. She wants to dance. She's in a hip-hop dance class.

The other girls are good. They can dance very well. Can Hanna dance very well? No, she can't. She trips and falls down. She makes mistakes. Hanna is sad.

"Mom, I don't want to dance," she says. "I'm a terrible dancer."

"You are not a terrible dancer," says Mom. "You need to practice."

Think

Do you agree with Hanna's mom? Why?

That night, Mom and Hanna read a story about a puppy. The puppy can't run. He trips and falls down. He makes mistakes. The puppy is sad.

Hip-hop Hanna

6.13

A horse shows the puppy how to run. The puppy practices and practices and practices. In the end, he can run *very* fast.

The teacher shows Hanna how to dance. Hanna practices and practices and practices.

Think

What happens next to Hanna?

One day, there's a school show.

In the show, Hanna dances *very* well.

Mom says, "Look at Hanna! She can dance really well now."

Everyone claps hard. They are clapping for Hanna!

Think

Why can Hanna dance so well now?

Explore the Text

1 Hanna practices a lot. What is the effect? Mark ✓ the correct answer.

She can't dance well. ☐

She can dance well. ☐

2 Read the story again. Color the correct answers.

a Hip-hop is a — dance. / movie.

b Hanna is sad because — she can't dance well. / she can't sing well.

c The puppy is sad because — he can't dance. / he can't run.

d Hanna's mom tells her — she's not a good dancer. / to practice.

3 Number the pictures in order. Retell the story with a partner.

☐

☐

☐

☐

How do you feel when you can't do something well?

Grammar: *Yes/No* Questions with *can* and *can't*

Can Hanna dance well?
Yes, she can. **No, she can't.**

1 6.14 **Listen to the song. Trace the correct answers.**

Susie can / can't dance,
But she can / can't run.
So we have lots of fun.

Tom can / can't walk,
But he can / can't play.
So he plays with me all day.

2 6.14 **Listen again and sing the song.**

3 **Look and ask your friends what they can do.**

drive

swim

roller-skate

read

Can you drive?

No, I can't.

Time to Talk!

Ask your classmates what their family members can do well.
Can your dad dance well?
Yes, he can. **No, he can't.**

1 6.15 Listen, point, and repeat.

1

tie

2

open

3

draw

4

find

5

say

6

spell

2 6.16 Listen to the conversations. Circle the answers.

Where is the girl?

a

b

Who helps her?

a

b

3 6.17 Listen and number.

Asking for Agreement

1 In groups, agree on three activities to do after school. Use the **Oracy Time!** expressions.

2 Complete **Check Your Oracy!** on Activity Book page 117.

Oracy Time!

Let's (play basketball). Do you agree?

Values AB page 116

What different things can we do?

Your challenge is to say what different abilities you have.

1. **Think** of three things you can do and three things you can't do.
2. **Make** a spinner. Draw a circle on paper. Divide it into six parts and write one action in each section.
3. **Draw** a picture next to each action.
4. **Cut** the circle out and glue it onto cardboard. Cut it out again.
5. **Draw** a small arrow on the cardboard. Cut it out and attach it to the spinner with a butterfly clip.
6. **Play** in pairs. Spin your partner's spinner and say if you can or can't do the action.

What can people do?
Look back through the unit. Share your ideas

AB pages 117–119

Oracy Performance Task 2: Discussion

1 What oracy skill are they practicing? Number the pictures.

1 Taking Turns | 2 Participating Actively | 3 Asking for Agreement

YOUR TASK

a 6.18 Listen and circle the correct activity on page 137.

b In small groups, discuss which activities on page 137 you can do to have fun.

c Agree on three activities to do together. Remember the ground rules for discussion.

charades

tag

musical chairs

freeze dance

hopscotch

hide-and-seek

board games

marbles

telephone

Check Your Oracy!

	☺	☺☺	☺☺☺
1 I listened to my classmates.			
2 I agreed or disagreed.			
3 I respected my classmates' opinions.			

7 Is all food healthy?

- ☐ **Talk** about the food you like and don't like.
- ☐ **Give** and respond to positive feedback.
- ☐ **Use** adjectives.
- ☐ **Make** a recipe for a dessert.
- ☐ **Go** shopping.

What are the children eating?

Do you like these foods?

Are these foods healthy?

1 ▶ 7.1 **Watch the video. Circle the food you see.**

fish

banana

watermelon

broccoli

2 ▶ 7.1 **Watch again. Complete the graphic organizer in the Activity Book.**

7.1

Key Words 1

fruit
banana
grapes
vegetable
spinach
sugar

AB page 122

Unit 7A Ready to Read: Nonfiction

Reading Strategy: Similarities and Differences

1 Categorize the food. Mark ✓ what is true.

	(orange)	(green)	vegetable	fruit
 orange	✓			✓
 carrot	✓		✓	
 spinach				
 grapes				

2 Say what is similar and what is different.

The orange is a fruit, but the carrot is a vegetable.

3 7.2 Listen, point, and repeat.

Anna / Noah

Anna / Noah

4 Compare the lunchboxes and circle the foods that are the same.

5 7.3 Listen. Whose lunchboxes are they? Circle the correct name.

7.4

Key Words 2

juice

water

oil

yogurt

tomato

rice

7.5

Snacks from Around the World!

Mexican Popsicles

Mexican popsicles are delicious. They're made from fruit, **juice**, and **water**. You put them in the freezer. You can also make them with **yogurt**.

Esteban from Mexico

Insects

Insects are a healthy snack. You can eat fried insects in Thailand. They are cooked in **oil**.

Aom from Thailand

7.6

Snacks from Around the World!

Plantains

Plantains are green bananas. They are cooked in oil. You can eat them in Cuba.

Lahmacun

Lahmacun is a Turkish snack. It has meat, tomatoes, and vegetables. It's delicious!

Hisao from Japan

Onigiri (Rice Balls)

Onigiri is a Japanese food. They are balls of white rice with seaweed.

Jake from Canada

Sandwiches

Sandwiches are a popular snack. They're made with bread. Are you hungry? You can make a sandwhich!

Think

Which foods in the pictures do you like? Which foods would you like to try?

1 Match the sentences to the children.

I like peanut butter sandwiches.

I like crickets.

I love popsicles.

I like onigiri with seaweed.

a

b

c

d

2 Draw the ingredients to complete the recipes. Are they similar or different?

Lahmacun

Popsicles

3 7.7 Key Words 3 Listen and repeat. Circle the words *freezer* and *fried* in the nonfiction text. Label the photos.

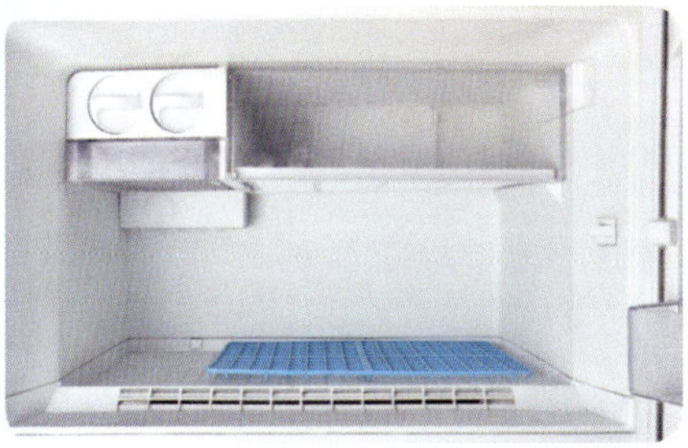

Which snacks from around the world are healthy?

4 Read and circle what is true for you.

I **like** / **don't like** vegetables.

I **like** / **don't like** meat.

Grammar in Context

Grammar: *like/don't like*

I **like** peanut butter sandwiches. I **don't like** cheese sandwiches.

1 7.8 Listen to the chant. What foods does the boy like? Mark ✓ or ✗.

2 Draw two foods you like and two you don't like.

I like ...

Mmm ... yum, yum, yum!

But I don't like ...

Yuck ... in my tum, tum, tum!

Time to Talk!

Say your chant to your partner.

I like bread. Mmm ... yum, yum, yum! But I don't like spinach. Yuck ... in my tum, tum, tum!

1 7.9 Listen, point, and repeat.

box

jam

cub

fox

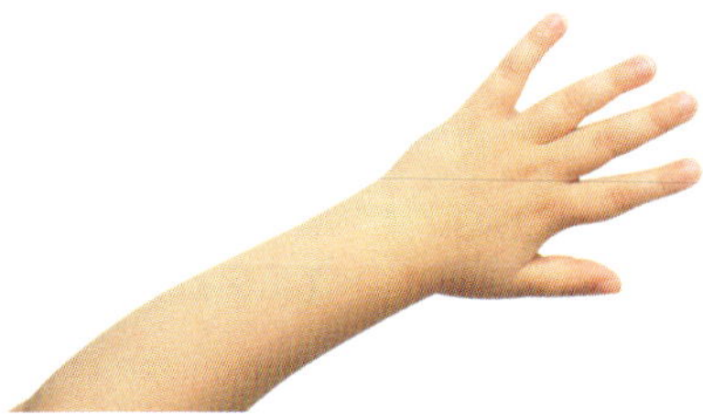
arm

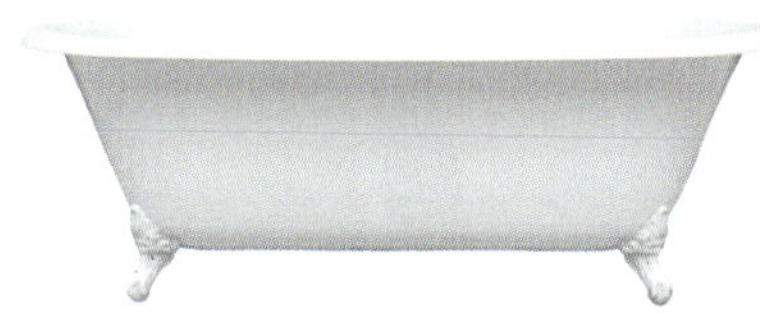
tub

2 7.10 Listen and say the chant.

The fox is in the box.
The fox is in the box.
Where's the fox?
It's in the box!

Where's the jam?
Where's the jam?
It's on my arm.
It's on my arm.

The cub is in the tub.
The cub is in the tub.
Where's the cub?
It's in the tub!

3 7.11 Listen and complete the words with *x*, *m*, or *b*.

a Look! It's a bear cu____!

b And over there is a fo____!

c I like ja____ on my bread.

d There is hot water in the tu____.

e Ouch! I hurt my ar____.

f Open the bo____.

Oracy Skill: Giving and Responding to Positive Feedback

1 ▶ 7.2 🎧 7.12 **Watch the video and answer the questions.**

a Who is giving a talk?
Kate / Emma

b What positive feedback does Kate receive?
Good job! / Please repeat that.

c How does Kate respond?
It's my turn. / Thank you.

d Do you like to receive positive feedback?
Yes / No

I love oranges. Oranges are fruit. This is a picture of orange jam.

Let's Practice Oracy! 9, 10

1. Prepare a presentation about your favorite fruit or vegetable.
2. Present your favorite fruit or vegetable to your class.
3. Remember to give and respond to positive feedback.

Check Your Oracy!

1 I spoke clearly.	**Yes / No**
2 I listened to my partner.	**Yes / No**
3 I said *Good job!* to my classmates.	**Yes / No**
4 I said *Thank you*.	**Yes / No**

Learn to Write: Adjectives

Adjectives describe people, places, or things.

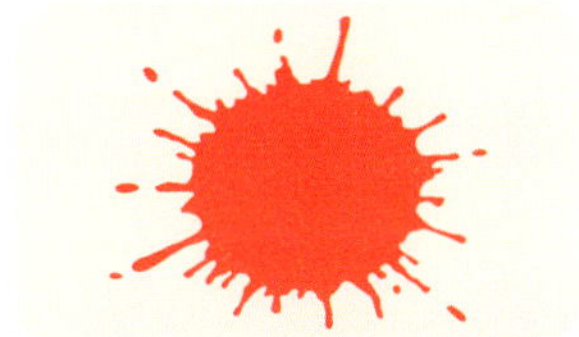

red

big

happy

three

1 Look and circle the adjectives.

a

two

balls

b

car

old

c

boy

angry

d

yellow

flower

2 Underline the adjectives and draw.

two big books

four yellow bananas

Time to Talk!

Game: Describe It!

1 Play in pairs.

2 Name a person, place, or thing.

3 Your partner describes it. Use some of the adjectives in the box.

Teacher!

One tall teacher.

short tall long old young
fast slow sad delicious

AB pages 129–30

Ready to Read: Fiction

1 7.13 Key Words 4 Listen, point, and repeat.

broccoli

fish

French fries

chocolate

soup

muffin

2 Which foods do you like? Use the key below to number the pictures in Activity 1.

3 7.14 Listen. Circle the things the girl likes in green and the things she doesn't like in red.

Reading Strategy: Main Idea

1 Look at the pictures from a story. Read the questions and trace the answers.

Stan Spinach

Bea Broccoli

Penny Peas

Zach Zucchini

a What are the pictures of? fruit vegetables

b What color are they? yellow green

c What is the story about? green vegetables
yellow vegetables

2 Look at the pictures from a story. What is the main idea? Circle.

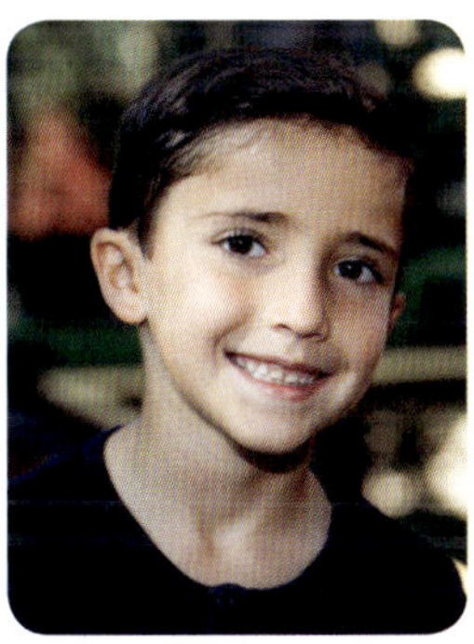
Alan

lunchbox

potato chips

candy

pizza

Alan's favorite snack Alan's unhealthy lunch Alan's healthy lunch

Draw what is inside your lunchbox. Is it healthy food?

7.15

No Broccoli, Please!

by Ángela Llanas

It's lunchtime. Yippee!

Billy likes fish.

Billy likes French fries.

Billy likes chocolate.

But Billy doesn't like broccoli! Yuck!
Billy pushes the broccoli away.

"Eat your broccoli," says Mom.

"I don't like broccoli," says Billy.

The telephone rings. It's Billy's grandma.

"We're eating lunch," Mom says. "Billy, eat your broccoli."

"I don't like broccoli," says Billy.

"What's that?" asks Grandma.

"Billy doesn't like broccoli!"

Think

How do you think Billy feels?

7.16

No Broccoli, Please!

On Sunday, Billy goes to his grandma's house to play with Fluffy, her dog.

"Lunchtime, Billy!" calls Grandma.

Grandma has a surprise. It's a little green dog.

"Hey, Fluffy," says Billy, "it looks just like you!"

Think

What is the green dog made of?

Grandma's soup is green and creamy.

"Mmm! I like pea soup," says Billy.

"Good," says Grandma. "There are chocolate muffins, too."

"I love chocolate muffins!"

When Billy's mom comes, Billy shows her the little dog.

"I made it out of broccoli," Grandma says.

"We had pea soup for lunch."

"It was *broccoli* soup," says Grandma.

Billy's surprised. "There were chocolate muffins, too."

"Chocolate and *broccoli* muffins," says Grandma. "The recipe is on the Internet!"

Billy's mom laughs. "So, Billy, do you like broccoli now?" she asks.

"Yes, I do!" says Billy.

Think

Do broccoli soup and pea soup taste the same?

Explore the Text

1 What is the main idea of the story? Circle the answer.

a Billy doesn't like broccoli.

b Muffins can be made with broccoli.

2 Number the pictures 1–4. Then, tell the story to a partner.

3 Read the text again. Trace the answers.

Billy: I like soup / pea soup.

Billy: I don't like chocolate / broccoli.

Billy eats chocolate broccoli muffins / chocolate muffins.

The dog's name is Billy / Fluffy.

Time to Talk!

Do chocolate broccoli muffins sound yummy or yucky?

What interesting or unusual foods can you name?

Insects are yucky.

Remember to take turns.

Grammar: *Yes/No* Questions with *like*

Do you like broccoli now? Yes, I do. / No, I don't.

1 7.17 **Listen to the chant. Color the answers.**

a Do you like muffins? Yes, I do. No, I don't.

b Do you like chocolate? Yes, I do. No, I don't.

c Do you like spinach? Yes, I do. No, I don't.

d Do you like broccoli? Yes, I do. No, I don't.

2 Trace the questions. Circle the answers that are true for you.

	You	Classmate
Do you like green  ?	Yes, I do. No, I don't.	Yes, I do.
Do you like  ?	Yes, I do. No, I don't.	
Do you like  ?	Yes, I do. No, I don't.	
Do you like  ?	Yes, I do. No, I don't.	
Do you like  ?	Yes, I do. No, I don't.	
Do you like  ?	Yes, I do. No, I don't.	

3 With a partner, ask the questions in Activity 2. Write the answers in the table.

Listening

1 **Look at the pictures. Which foods are unhealthy?**

cookies

broccoli

French fries

spinach

donuts

zucchini

pizza

green beans

2 7.18 **Listen to the song. Circle the main idea.**

a yummy junk food b junk food vs. healthy food c healthy vegetables

3 **Circle the junk food in Activity 1 that is mentioned in the song.**

4 7.18 **Listen again and circle.**

Healthy food makes you …

grow

slow

Junk food makes you …

weak

strong

? **Is it OK to eat some junk food?**

Values AB page 136

How can we make a healthy dessert?

Your challenge is to make a recipe for a healthy dessert!

1. **Search** for an easy recipe for a healthy dessert with a partner.
2. **Make** a list of the food you need. Write how much you need. For example: 1 cup of yogurt.
3. **Write** and **draw** the recipe. Draw pictures of the ingredients and the measuring tools you need. (spoon, cup)
4. **Present** your recipe to the class.

Remember to give positive feedback and respond to it. Complete **Check Your Oracy!** in the Activity Book.

Is all food healthy?
Look back through the unit and share your ideas.

AB pages 137–39

SPEAKING MISSION

Go to the store and buy some groceries.

Before Your Mission

1 7.19 Listen, point, and repeat.

bread

cookies

lollipop

potato chips

tomato

corn

2 Circle the healthy foods in green. Circle the unhealthy foods in red.

3 Look and say the name of each food item.

a

b

c

d

e

f

Time to Talk!

Play Draw and Guess.

Is it a tomato?

Yes, it is!

During Your Mission

4 7.20 **Listen. What does the boy buy?**

5 **Go shopping!**

a Write prices for the items in the store.
b Choose three things to buy.
c In pairs, role-play buying.

Key Language

Can I have a lollipop, please?
Can I have two oranges, please?
Here you go.
How much is it?
It's one dollar.
Thank you!

What foods can you buy at a local market? Are they healthy?

8 Are routines important?

- Talk about daily routines.
- Learn to speak up.
- Identify statements.
- Make a poster with your routines.
- Assign tasks in the classroom.

What is a routine?

What are the children doing?

Do you have similar routines?

8.1

Key Words 1

brush my teeth
eat breakfast
go to school
walk
ride my bike
take the bus

1 8.1 **Watch the video. Circle the routines you see.**

2 8.1 **Watch again. Complete the graphic organizer in the Activity Book.**

AB page 142

Ready to Read: Nonfiction

Reading Strategy: Summarizing

1 Read the text. Then, point to the queen bee.

I am a honeybee.
My mother is the queen. She is very big!
I work with my sisters. I am busy all day.

I help the queen.

I collect food.

I make honey.

I clean my home.

2 Circle the best summary of the text.

a The text is about a honeybee and all the things she does.

b The text is about a bee's home.

Is the bee's routine important?

8.2

Key Words 2

sleep

do exercise

have fun

take a bath

change clothes

wash my hands

8.3

Henry's Healthy Habits

Hi! I'm Henry. These are things I do to stay healthy!

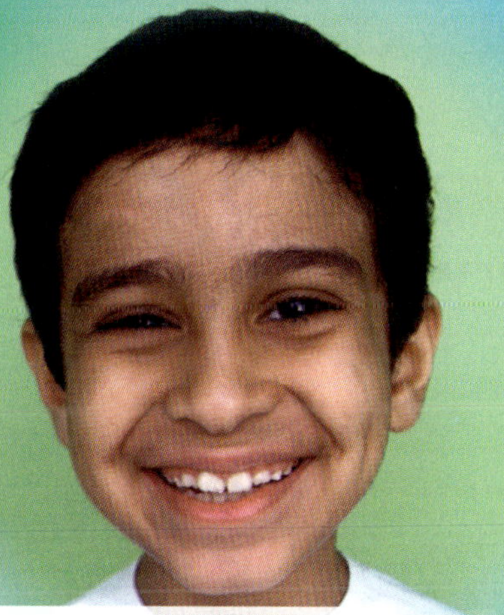

1 Sleep 9 to 11 hours every night.

Sleep is very important. I **sleep** 10 hours every night.

2 Do exercise.

I like to **do exercise**. I play baseball at school!

3 Have fun!

After school, I ride my bike or play tag with my friends. I always **have fun**!

8.4 Henry's Healthy Habits

4 Keep clean.

I **take a bath** every day.

I **change my clothes** when they are dirty.

I brush my teeth twice a day— in the morning and at night.

I **wash my hands** …

after I use the bathroom.

before I eat.

Dinner's ready!

after I play outside.

after I play with animals.

Why is keeping clean an important routine?

Think

Why do we wash our hands?

5 Eat healthy food.

Breakfast is very important. I always eat fruit and drink milk for breakfast. Then, I have lots of energy for school.

Explore the Text

8A

1 Read the text again. Mark ✓ the correct summary.

- [ ] This text is about Henry's healthy routines.
- [ ] This text is about Henry's favorite routines.

2 Match the healthy advice to what Henry says.

1 Sleep 9 to 11 hours.	a I sleep 10 hours every night.
2 Do exercise.	b I always eat fruit.
3 Have fun!	c I take a bath every day.
4 Keep clean.	d I play with my friends after school.
5 Eat healthy food.	e I play baseball at school.

3 8.5 Key Words 3 **Listen and repeat. Circle the words *before* and *after* in the nonfiction text. What do you do *before* and *after* you eat breakfast? Label the pictures.**

a

____

eat breakfast

b

____

Time to Talk!

What do you do before and after school?
Before school, I eat breakfast.

Remember to listen to others.

Grammar in Context

Grammar: Present Simple: Affirmative

I **wash** my hands. I **sleep** ten hours a day.

1 8.6 Listen to the song. Number the pictures.

I brush my teeth. ☐

I stretch and stretch. 1

I play with my friends. ☐

I eat eggs and toast. ☐

2 8.6 Sing the song. Act out the actions as you sing!

3 What things do you do every day? Tell a classmate.

Before I go to school, I ...

After school, I ...

What are your healthy habits?
I brush my teeth in the morning.

1 8.7 Listen, point, and repeat.

desk

fast

ant

mask

nest

cent

2 8.8 Listen to the chant and point to the words in Activity I.

3 8.8 Listen again and say the chant.

4 Complete the words with *sk*, *st*, or *nt*. Then, number.

1 Look at the little black a__________.

2 The bird is in its ne__________.

3 He is wearing a funny ma__________.

4 She rides her bike fa__________!

5 I'm sitting at my de__________.

6 It costs one ce__________!

Oracy Skill: Speaking Up

1 8.2 8.9 **Watch the video. Then, watch again and answer the questions.**

a Who is giving a talk? **Jack** **Liam**

b The class can't understand Jack at first. Why?

He isn't speaking up. **He is speaking too loudly.**

c Circle the phrases Jack's classmates say.

I don't understand. **It's my turn.** **Please repeat that.**

d Does Jack speak up at the end of his talk? **Yes / No**

Let's Practice Oracy! 4, II

1. Prepare a talk about your routine before school or after school.
2. Work in pairs. Remember to speak up.
3. Listen to your partner's talk. Ask your partner to repeat if necessary.

Check Your Oracy!

1 I talked about my routine.	Yes / No
2 I spoke up.	Yes / No
3 I asked my partner to repeat.	Yes / No

Learn to Write: Statements

A statement is a sentence. A statement tells us something.

I play sports.

I wash my hands.

1 **Circle the statements. Match them with the pictures.**

I take the bus to school.

Is it a school bus?

I brush my teeth every day.

my teeth

a

b

2 **Read and draw.**

I eat a sandwich in the morning.

I play the piano every day.

Time to Talk!

In pairs, answer the question.

What do you do every day?

I read books and I play with my friends.

AB pages 149–50

Ready to Read: Fiction

1 8.10 Key Words 4 Listen, point, and repeat.

wake up

collect

march

find

carry

clean

2 Read and number the pictures.

1 I can't **find** my ...
2 I **clean** my ...
3 I **wake up** at ...
4 I **march** in ...
5 I **collect** ...
6 I **carry** my ...

parades.

dolls.

book.

ten.

1 schoolbag.

bedroom.

Reading Strategy: Making Judgments

1 Look at the pictures. Which breakfast is healthy?

a

b

2 Look and circle ✓ or ✗.

a
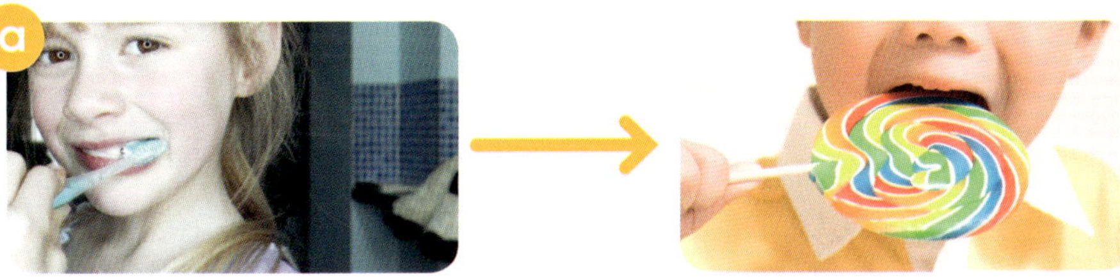
brush teeth → eat candy ✓ ✗

b
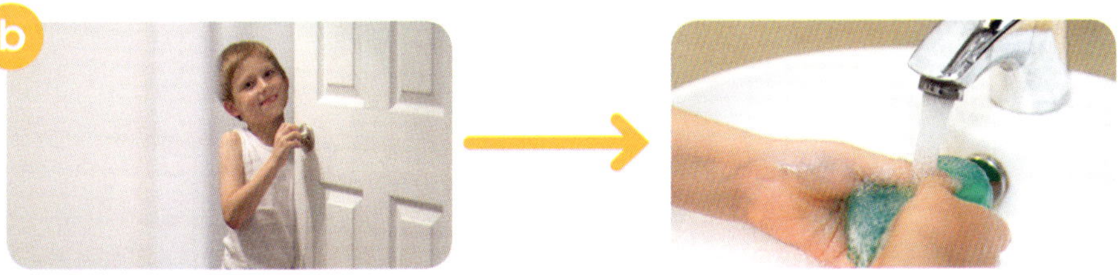
go to bathroom → wash hands ✓ ✗

c

play with friends → do homework ✓ ✗

d
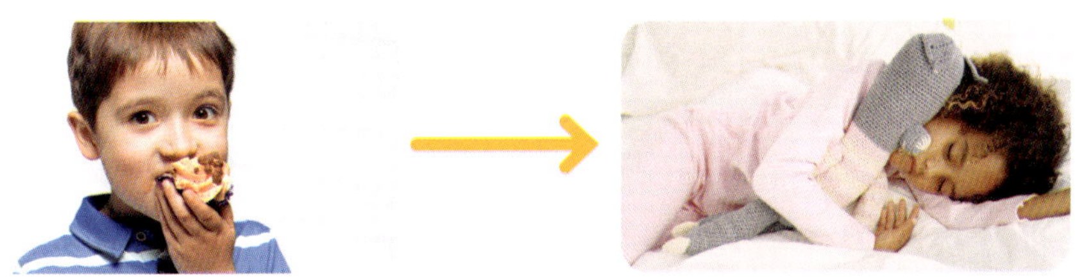
eat chocolate → go to bed ✓ ✗

Andy Ant

by Silvia Zapiain

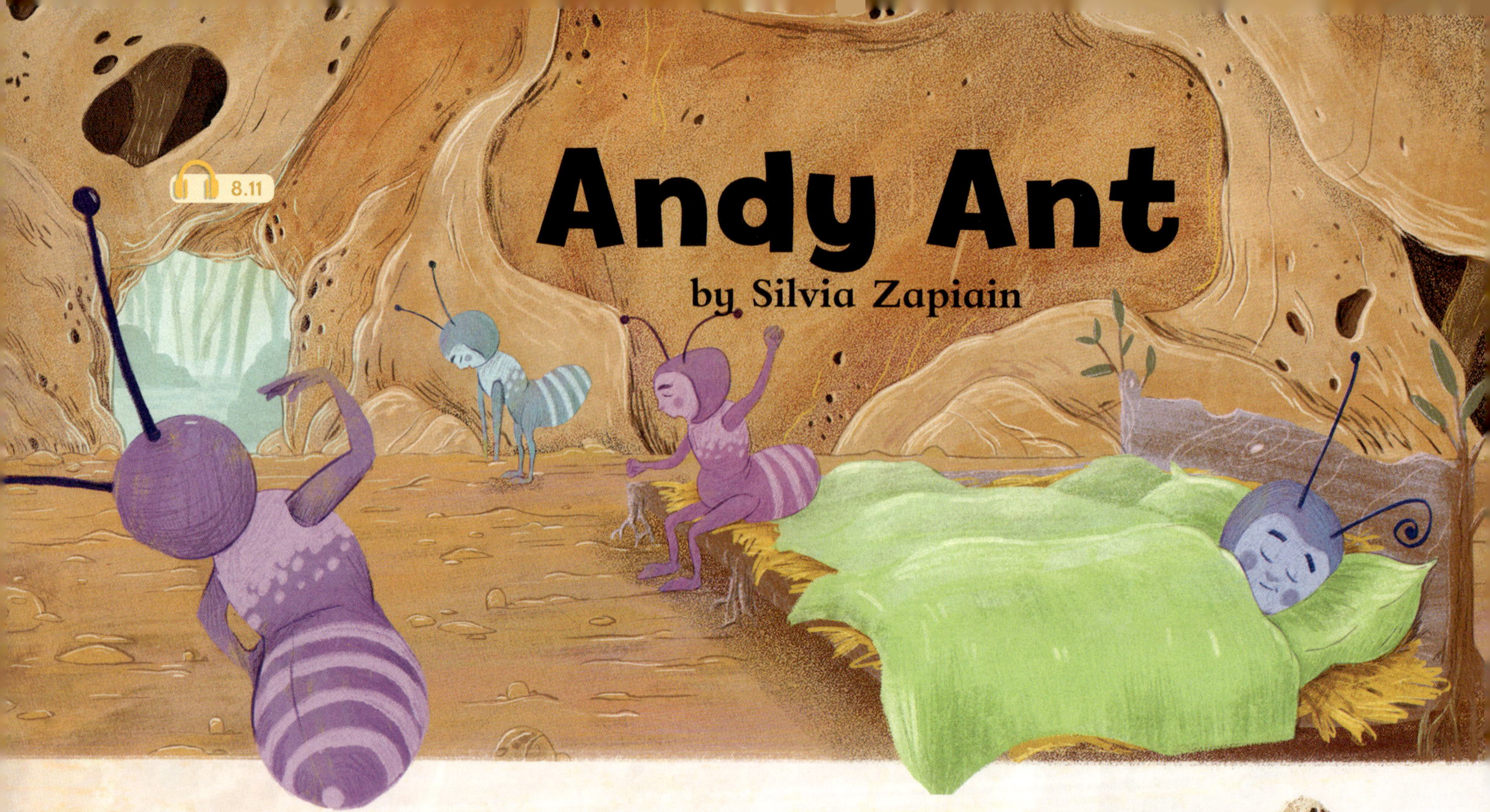

"Wake up, little ants!" says Mom.

"It's Monday morning! Let's collect bread crumbs."

"Coming, Mom!" say the little ants.

So, off they go, leaving Andy Ant sleeping tight.

The next day, Mom says, "Wake up, little ants!"

"It's Tuesday morning! Let's march!"

"Coming, Mom!" say the little ants.

So, off they go, leaving Andy Ant sleeping tight.

Think

Why do you think Andy Ant is sleeping?

The next day, Mom says, "Wake up, little ants!

It's Wednesday morning! Let's find seeds!"

"Coming, Mom!" say the little ants.

So, off they go, leaving Andy Ant sleeping tight.

The next day, Mom says, "Wake up, little ants!

It's Thursday morning! Let's carry leaves!"

"Coming, Mom!" say the little ants.

So, off they go, leaving Andy Ant sleeping tight.

Think

How do you think Andy Ant's brothers and sisters feel?

8.12

Andy Ant

The next day, Mom says, "Wake up, little ants! It's Friday morning! Let's clean the house!"

"Coming, Mom!" say the little ants.

So, off they go, leaving Andy Ant sleeping tight.

Think

Why do you think Andy Ant doesn't help?

The next morning, Andy Ant is up early.
"I don't sleep late on Saturdays!" says Andy.
"I'm ready," he says. "I'm ready to help."
"I'm ready to collect bread crumbs."
"I'm ready to march."
"I'm ready to find seeds."
"I'm ready to carry leaves."
"I'm ready to clean the house!"
"But, Andy," says Mom. "It's Saturday!"
"We don't work on Saturdays!
Today we all go out and play!"

Think

Does Andy Ant help his mom on Saturday? Why?

Explore the Text

1 Match what the ants do with the days of the week.

Monday Tuesday Wednesday Thursday Friday Saturday

2 Number the pictures in order. Retell the story in groups.

3 How do you think Mom feels about Andy Ant in each situation? Look and circle.

a

b

Do you think Andy Ant has a good attitude? Why or why not?

Grammar: Present Simple: Negative

I **don't sleep** on Saturdays!

We **don't work** on Saturdays.

1 8.13 **Listen and mark ✓ the things the girl talks about.**

2 8.13 **Listen again. Complete the sentences with the verbs.**

make brush eat play eat wear

a I don't ______________ cake.

b I don't ______________ with snakes.

c I don't ______________ red.

d I don't ______________ my bed.

e I don't ______________ pears.

f I don't ______________ my hair.

Time to Talk!

Tell a partner what you don't do each day of the week.

On Mondays, I don't watch TV.

Listening

1 8.14 **Listen and circle the correct answer.**

The conversations are about … **the things we do every day.** / **our favorite things.**

2 8.14 **Listen again. Number the activities in order.**

Abby's Morning Routine

make the bed

brush hair

eat breakfast

get dressed

brush teeth

Dale's Bedtime Routine

go to bed

eat a snack

brush teeth

take a bath

read a story

3 **Draw your morning or bedtime routine on Sundays.**

Time to Talk!

Tell a partner your routine on Sunday morning.

On Sundays, I get up and play with my toys.

Values AB page 156

How can we describe our routines?

Your challenge is to make a poster to show your routine.

1. **Choose** a day of the week. Then, decide on a morning, afternoon, or bedtime routine.
2. **Think** about the things you do.
3. **Draw** pictures or download images from the Internet that show the things you do. Glue them onto a large sheet of paper in the order you do them. Use arrows to show the sequence.
4. **Display** your poster and describe your routine to the class.

Are routines important?
Look back through the unit. Share your ideas.

AB pages 157–59

SPEAKING MISSION

Assign tasks to follow a class routine.

Before Your Mission

1 8.15 **Listen, point, and repeat.**

take attendance

raise your hand

stand up / sit down

open your books

eat lunch

be quiet

take out / put away

draw

spell

2 8.16 **Listen and point to the actions in Activity 1.**

3 8.16 **Listen again and do the actions.**

Time to Talk!

Play Simon Says.

Simon says, stand up!

During Your Mission

4 8.17 **Listen. Mark ✓ the actions you hear.**

a

b

c

d

e

f

g

5 **Imagine you are the teacher. In your notebooks, make a list of six classroom activities for your class.**

6 **In small groups, take turns role-playing the teacher.**

Key Language

Hello, I'm (Ms./Mr. Brown).
(Sit down), please.
First, (open your book).
Let's (read).
Now, (stand up), please.
What do we do next?
Let's go to the playground.

? Are school routines important? Why?

9 Why do we wear different clothes?

- ☐ **Talk** about the clothes people wear.
- ☐ **Learn** to stand up straight when giving a talk.
- ☐ **Identify** questions.
- ☐ **Make** a jigsaw puzzle.
- ☐ **Give** a final presentation.

What are the children wearing?

Why are their clothes different?

Do you ever wear any of these clothes? When?

9.1

Key Words 1

clothes
cold
jacket
hot
T-shirt
shoes

1 9.1 **Watch the video. Circle the clothes mentioned.**

 T-shirt	 skirt	 sweater	 shoes
 boots	 mittens	 hat	 jacket

2 9.1 **Watch again. Complete the graphic organizer in the Activity Book.**

AB page 162

Unit 9A Ready to Read: Nonfiction

Reading Strategy: Cause and Effect

Cause → Effect

1 Look at the pictures. Write *C* (cause) or *E* (effect).

a

C

b

2 Draw the effect.

Cause → Effect

? What do you wear when it's hot?

9.2

Key Words 2

wear

hat

skirt

pants

gloves

dress

9.3

Traditional Clothes from *Around the World*

Every country has traditional clothes. People **wear** them at special times. Traditional clothes are very important. They are part of who we are.

In the mountains of Peru, it's cold. Brrr ... People wear warm, colorful clothes. They are made of wool from alpacas. Look at the boy's clothes! What is he wearing?

Here is an Inuit boy. He's from Canada. What is he wearing?

I'm wearing **gloves**, a warm jacket, and boots. They are made of fur.

9.4

Traditional Clothes from *Around the World*

In Norway, people wear traditional clothes, too. These clothes are called a "bunad." They wear these clothes for special celebrations.

Look at the girl's clothes. She's wearing a **skirt** made of wool. She's also wearing a special hat. The boy's wearing a red vest, a white shirt, **pants**, and a hat.

In India, it's very hot. In this photo, the girl is wearing a sari. It's a long **dress**. And the boy? He isn't wearing a sari, he's wearing a shirt called a tunic. These clothes are made of silk. Silk feels cool when it's hot.

In other hot places, people wear big hats or turbans. They protect you from the sun.

I'm not wearing a hat. I'm wearing a turban!

Think

What are the traditional clothes in your country?

1 Circle *Yes* or *No*.

a Ponchos are long dresses. **Yes / No**
b In India, girls wear saris. **Yes / No**
c In Norway, people wear ponchos. **Yes / No**
d Hats protect you from the sun. **Yes / No**

2 Look at the photos. What do people wear for each kind of weather? Match the words to the photos.

It's cold!

a 

It's hot!

b 

gloves jacket sari boots

turban T-shirt tunic

3 9.5 Key Words 3 Listen and repeat. Circle the words *wool* and *cool* in the nonfiction text. Label the pictures.

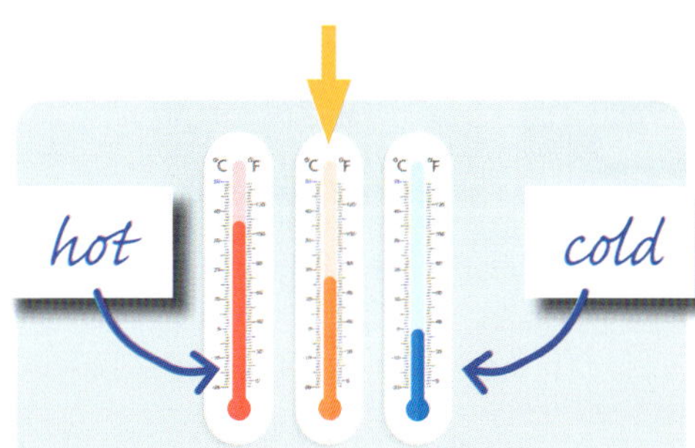

_______________ _______________

? What are your favorite clothes when it's cold?

Grammar: Present Continuous: Affirmative and Negative

I'm wearing gloves and big boots.
She's wearing a long skirt.

I'm not wearing a hat.
He's not wearing a jacket.

1 9.6 Listen to the chant. Match the words to the correct child.

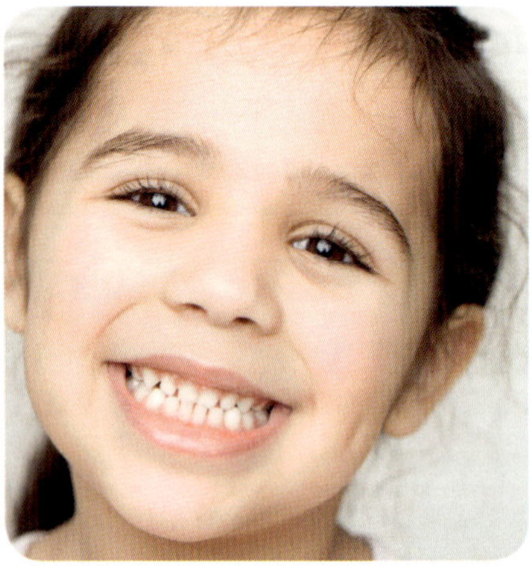

hot cold
gloves hat
dress jacket

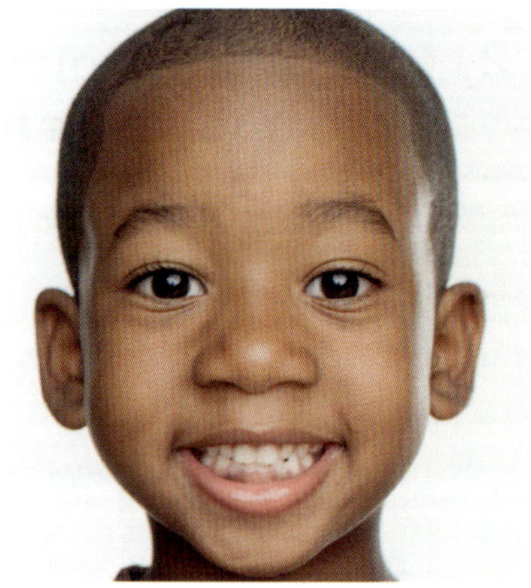

2 Look at the pictures. Trace the answers.

Girl:

I am / am not wearing shoes.

I am / am not wearing boots.

Boy:

I am / am not wearing a T-shirt.

I am / am not wearing a jacket.

Time to Talk!

Draw a boy or girl on a piece of paper. Clearly draw and color his or her clothing. Place the drawing face down on a table. Take turns choosing a drawing and describing the clothes.

1 9.7 **Listen, point, and repeat.**

grow

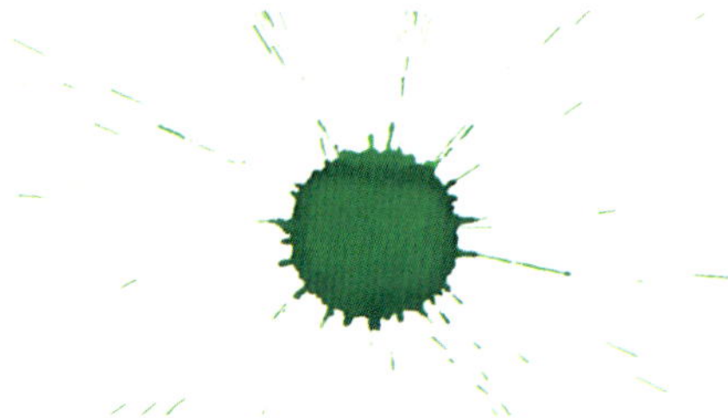

green

grandma

plant

play

plum

2 9.8 **Listen and follow along. Then sing the song.**

Grandma's Plant Grows

Grandma's green plant
Grows and grows.
Come and see,
One, two, three.

Grandma's green plant
Grows into a tree, into a tree.
Come and see,
One, two, three.

Grandma's green plant
Grows into a plum tree, into a plum tree.
Come and see,
One, two, three.

Come climb and play with me
in Grandma's big plum tree!

3 **Go through the book and find words starting with *gr* and *pl*.**

Oracy

Oracy Skill: Standing Up Straight and Keeping Still

1 9.2 9.9 **Watch the video and circle the correct answers.**

a Who is not standing up straight? **Kate / Liam**

b Who is not standing still at first? **Kate / Liam**

c Whose presentation is easier to understand? **Kate's / Liam's**

2 9.2 9.9 **Watch the video again and circle the phrase you hear.**

This is … I like …

Let's Practice Oracy! I, I2

1 Prepare a presentation about your favorite clothes.

2 Draw pictures for your presentation.

3 Give your presentation to your classmates.

These are my favorite clothes. This is my favorite dress.

Check Your Oracy!

1 I gave a presentation in front of my class.	**Yes / No**
2 I stood still.	**Yes / No**
3 I stood up straight.	**Yes / No**

Ready to Write

Learn to Write: Questions

What color is the skirt? Do you like my shoes?

1 Underline the questions. Then match them to the answers.

1 She's eight.

2 Can you ride a bike?

3 What's your favorite color?

4 It's blue.

5 I'm wearing a T-shirt.

6 No, I can't.

7 How old is she?

a

Eight.

b

Blue.

c

No.

2 Complete the questions.

How old ____________________? I'm 7.

Can you ____________________? Yes, I can.

Time to Talk!

Have a class competition. The teacher sets the clock for five minutes.

In small teams, write as many questions as you can.

The team that writes the most questions correctly is the winner.

Unit 9B Ready to Read: Fiction

1 9.10 Key Words 4 **Listen, point, and repeat.**

emperor

thief

palace

expensive

smart

fool

2 **Find and circle what you see that represents the words from Activity 1.**

3 **What is missing from the illustration in Activity 2? Write the word.**

____

Reading Strategy: Beginning, Middle, and End

Beginning → Middle → End

1 **Read the story. Number the beginning (1), middle (2), and end (3).**

It's very cold. Where is Johnny's jacket? Oh, no!
His favorite jacket is too small.

Johnny and Mom go to the store. Johnny likes a red jacket.
Red is his favorite color.

His mom buys the jacket. His new jacket is warm!

2 9.11 **Listen to the story and draw the end.**

Do we all like the same kinds of clothes? Why or why not?

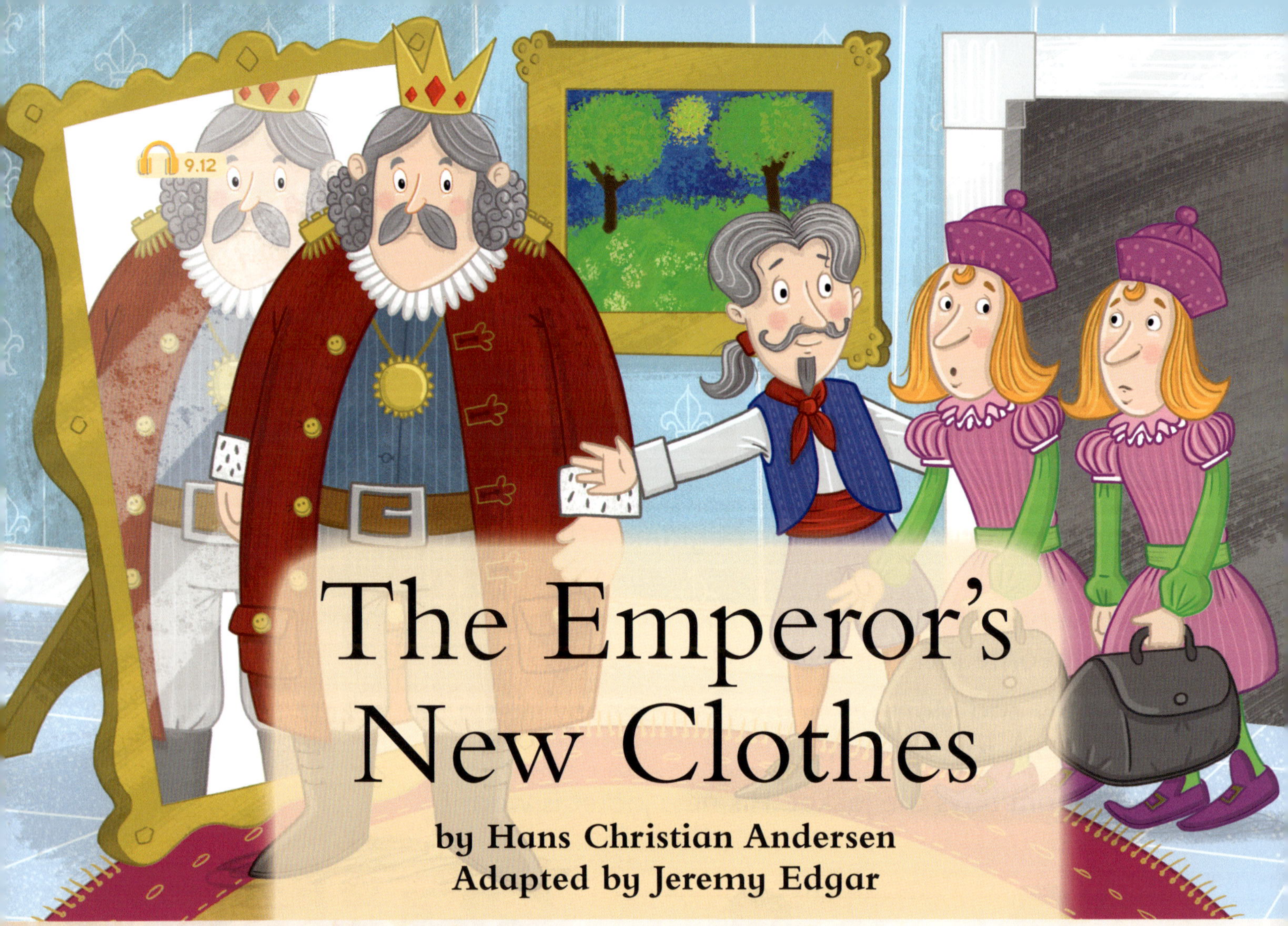

The Emperor's New Clothes

by Hans Christian Andersen
Adapted by Jeremy Edgar

This is the Emperor. He loves clothes. Every day, he buys new clothes—red clothes, blue clothes, purple clothes, green clothes, even gold clothes!

One day, two thieves go to the palace.

"We have magic clothes!" they tell the Emperor.

"Are you wearing magic clothes?" the Emperor asks one of the thieves.

"No, I'm not. They're too expensive."

"Really?" says the Emperor.

"Yes, because only very smart people can see them," the thieves say. "Fools can't."

"Show me the magic clothes!" the Emperor says.

The thieves hold up the clothes. But there is nothing there.

The Emperor is worried. "Am I a fool?" he asks himself.

"Oh, those clothes look magnificent!" the Emperor says.

"I want to buy them."

Think

Can the Emperor see the clothes?

9.13

The Emperor's New Clothes

The Emperor calls his minister.

The minister is surprised. "Are you wearing your new clothes?" he asks.

"Yes, I am," the Emperor says.

He tells the minister about the magic.

The minister doesn't see anything.

"Those clothes look wonderful!" he says.

"Show them to the people. Have a parade!"

Think

Can the minister see the clothes?

Everyone is at the parade.

One boy shouts, "What is the Emperor wearing?"

"I'm wearing my magic clothes," the Emperor says.

"But I can only see underwear!" the boy laughs.

"It's true!" the people shout. They all laugh.

The Emperor is embarrassed. He will never wear his "magic" clothes again.

Think

Is the boy smart or a fool? Why?

Explore the Text

1 Circle *Yes* or *No*.

a Are the magic clothes expensive? **Yes / No**

b The emperor can see the magic clothes. **Yes / No**

c The minister can see the magic clothes. **Yes / No**

d The boy is a fool. **Yes / No**

2 Number the beginning (1), middle (2), and end (3) of the story.

☐ The emperor is worried. "Am I a fool?" he asks himself.

☐ "We have magic clothes!" they tell the Emperor.

☐ "But I can only see underwear!" the boy says.

3 Number the pictures in order. Retell the story in pairs.

What are you wearing?
What color are your clothes?

Remember to speak up so that others can hear you.

Grammar: Present Continuous: *Yes/No* Questions

Are you wearing magic clothes? Yes, I am.

Are you wearing your new clothes? No, I'm not.

1 9.14 **Listen to the chant. Mark ✓ the clothes and colors you hear.**

☐ skirt

☐ shirt

☐ blue

☐ red

2 9.14 **Listen again. Complete the questions and the answers.**

a Are you wearing a __________ today? Yes, I __________.

b Are you wearing __________ today? No, __________.

3 **Make new verses for the chant.**

Time to Talk!

Draw a picture of yourself wearing your favorite clothes. Your partner guesses what you are wearing.

Are you wearing a T-shirt?

No, I'm not.

Listening

1 Listen. Who likes their school uniform?

Holly

Wayne

2 Listen again and mark ✓ the clothes Holly and Wayne mention.

	Holly	Wayne
 tie	✓	
 skirt		
 shorts		
 hat		

	Holly	Wayne
 shirt		
 coat		
 socks		

Stand Up Straight and Keep Still

1 Draw what you usually wear to school. Then, draw what you usually wear after school.
2 In groups, take turns describing the clothes you wear.
At school, I wear a blue skirt and a white shirt.
3 Remember to stand up straight and keep still while you are talking.
4 Complete **Check Your Oracy!** on Activity Book page 177.

Values AB page 176

How do we dress for special occasions?

Your challenge is to make a jigsaw puzzle about clothes for special occasions.

1. **Talk** about the clothes you wear on special occasions.
2. **Choose** your favorite special occasion. For example: your birthday, a festival, or a holiday.
3. **Look for** a photograph or draw a person wearing special clothes for the occasion.
4. **Cut** the photo or drawing into pieces to make a jigsaw puzzle.
5. **Give** your puzzle to a partner to put together.
6. **Describe** to your partner the clothes the person is wearing.

Why do we wear different clothes?
Look back through the unit. Share your ideas.

AB pages 177–79

Oracy Performance Task 3: Presentation

1 **Read and number the pictures.**

1 Giving and Receiving Positive Feedback **2 Speaking Up**

3 Standing up Straight and Keeping Still

2 **Read and match the speech bubbles to the two options.**

Please repeat that.

I don't understand.

Good job!

Thank you!

Giving and Receiving Positive Feedback

Speaking Up

YOUR TASK

a Prepare to give a final presentation.

b Draw pictures for each category on page 203. You can look back through your book.

c Choose a category and plan your presentation. Draw pictures on a separate piece of paper.

d Give your 1- to 2-minute presentation to your class.

All About Me	My Favorite Toy
My Bedroom	My Favorite Wild Animal
My Favorite Foods	My Routine
My Clothes	My Friends

Check Your Oracy!

	☺	☺☺	☺☺☺
1 I planned my presentation.			
2 I stood up straight and kept still.			
3 I spoke up.			
4 I gave positive feedback to my classmates.			

MY CREATIVE JOURNAL

Cambridge Primary Path

Foundation

BY PAUL DRURY

CAMBRIDGE UNIVERSITY PRESS

CAMBRIDGE
UNIVERSITY PRESS

University Printing House, Cambridge CB2 8BS, United Kingdom

One Liberty Plaza, 20th Floor, New York, NY 10006, USA

477 Williamstown Road, Port Melbourne, VIC 3207, Australia

Torre de los Parques, Colonia Tlacoquemécatl del Valle, Mexico City CP 03200, Mexico

314–321, 3rd Floor, Plot 3, Splendor Forum, Jasola District Centre, New Delhi – 10025, India

103 Penang Road, #05-06/07, Visioncrest Commercial, Singapore 238467

Cambridge University Press is part of the University of Cambridge.

It furthers the University's mission by disseminating knowledge in the pursuit of education, learning and research at the highest international levels of excellence.

www.cambridge.org
Information on this title: www.cambridge.org/9781108709941

First published 2019

20 19 18 17

Printed in Poland by Opolgraf

A catalogue record for this publication is available from the British Library

ISBN 978-1-108-70993-4 Student's Book Foundation Level
ISBN 978-1-108-72689-4 Student's Book with Creative Journal Foundation Level

Additional resources for this publication at
www.cambridge.org/primarypath

THIS IS WHAT HAPPENS WHEN YOU USE THIS BOOK.

CONTENTS

WHAT'S MY NAME?

WRITE YOUR NAME. WRITE IT **REALLY** BIG.

FILL IN THE COLORS.

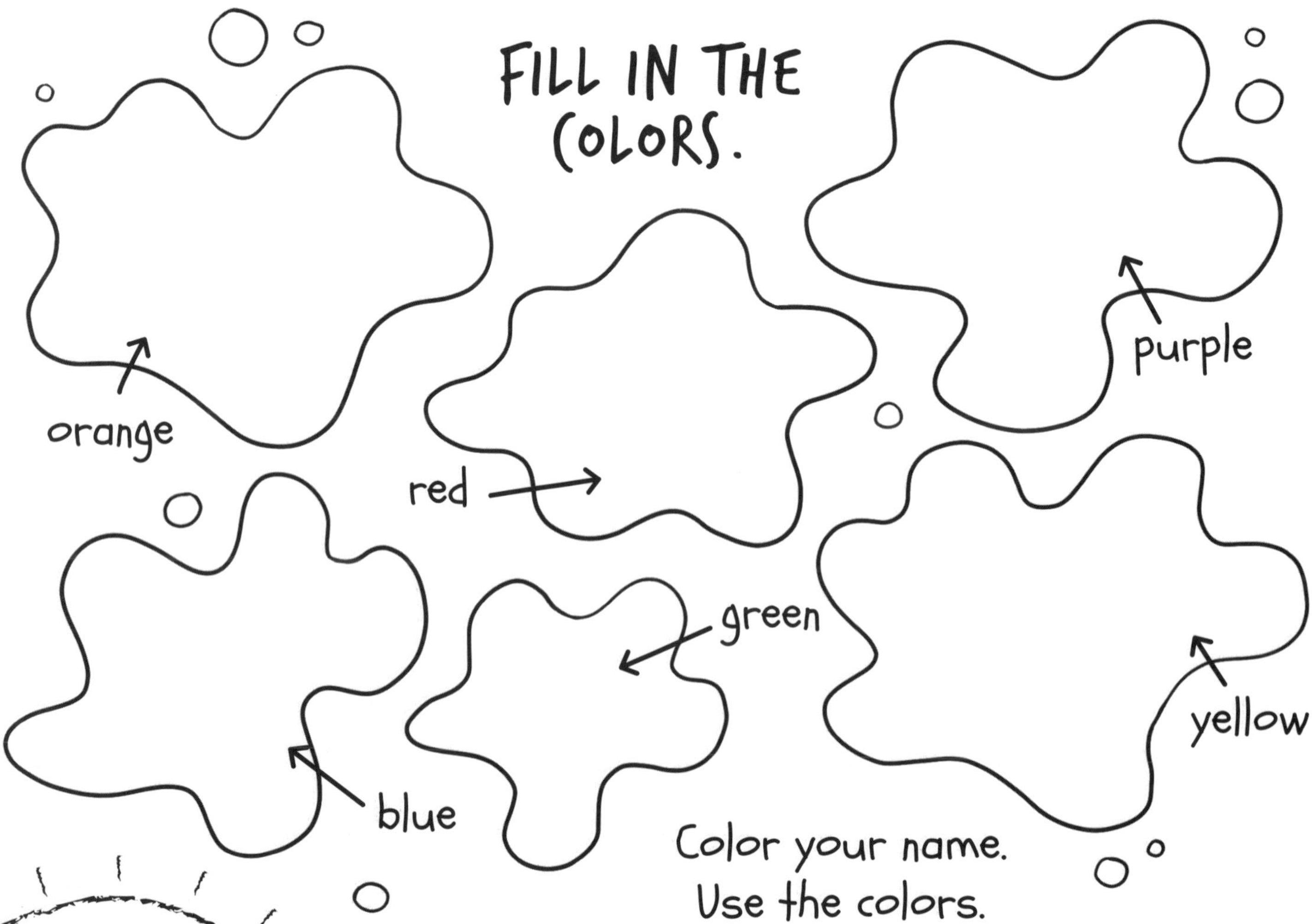

Color your name.
Use the colors.

CAN YOU COMPLETE ALL THE TASKS?

1. Write your name really small ....

2. How many fingers do you have? ....

3. How many feet do you have? ....

4. Give names to all your fingers.

5. Write “mouth” backwards h..

6. What’s 4 + 3? ....

7. What’s 4 – 3? ....

8. What’s your favorite color? ....

9. What’s your favorite number? ....

1 WHO AM I?

CAN YOU SPOT THE DIFFERENCES?

WRITE S FOR SAME OR D FOR DIFFERENT.

MEET THE ALPHABET

Decorate all the letters of the alphabet. Draw and color.

GRANDMA TURTLE SURFER

DECORATE GRANDMA'S SHELL. DRAW AND COLOR.

THE PENGUIN WANTS TO BE A HUMAN

This penguin wants to look like a little boy or girl. Draw and color.

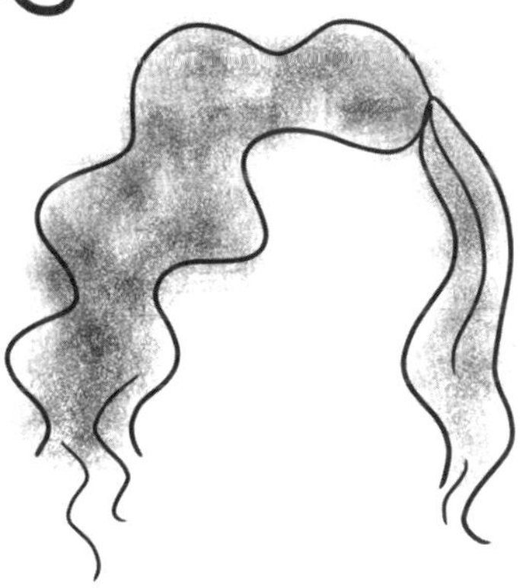

What color are the penguin's eyes?

2 WHAT IS SCHOOL?

MY CLASSMATES

Think of your classmates.
Draw circles with faces.

Max

How many classmates can you remember?

MY SCHOOL

Put your pencil on START HERE. Close your eyes. Draw the route to the bathroom, the gym, and the playground.

THAT'S NOT MY BACKPACK

Find and circle your backpack.

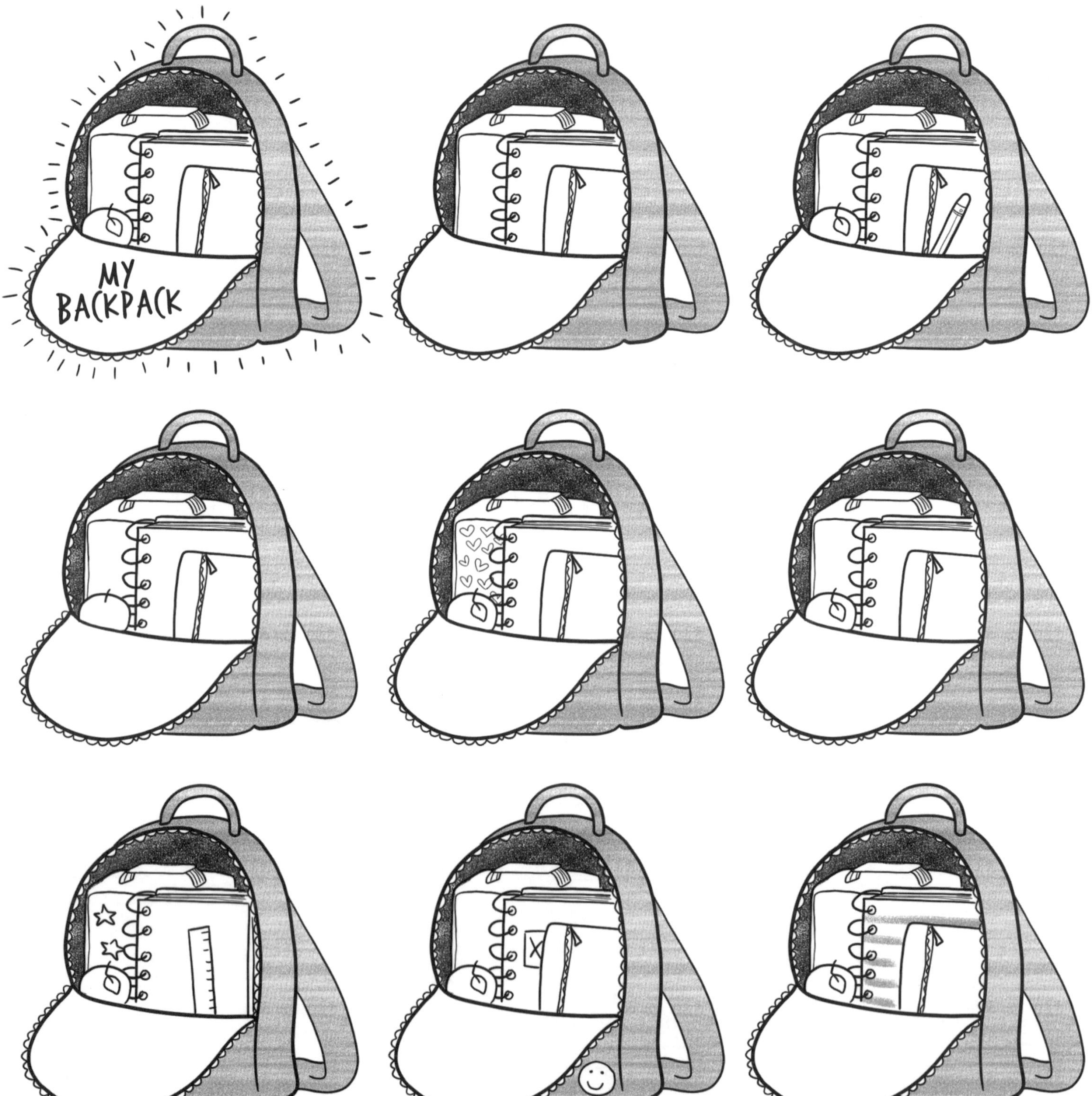

I CAN'T FIND MY THINGS.

Find and circle your things in the classroom.

3 WHAT IS A TOY?

PLAY WITH ME!

Draw lines from one toy to another.

Can you add more lines?

Now, decorate the shapes.

FINGERPRINT FUN

Cover the page with your fingerprints.
Then, decorate each one.

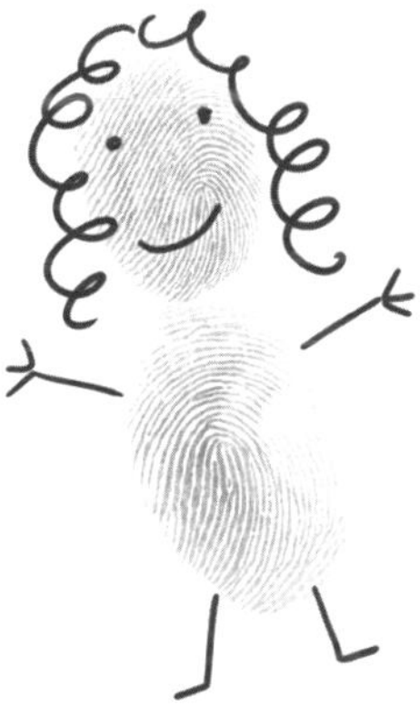

DOES YOUR BRAIN TALK TO YOUR HAND?

FOLLOW THE INSTRUCTIONS.

Color this green. → **red**

green

↑ Color this red.

Point to a word. Ask your friend to say the word. Then, point to a word and ask your friend to say the color.

Rub your hand on your head in circles and draw a robot. Use a circle, a square, and a triangle. Don't stop rubbing!

ART WITH AN ERASER

Gently color in each section with the side of your pencil. Draw toys and make patterns using your eraser.

CREATIVE BLAST 1

FLOW

LET YOUR PENCIL FOLLOW THE FLOW.

Put on some music. Continue the lines. Make interesting shapes!

FOCUS

TEST YOUR MEMORY

1. Look at the picture.
2. Cover the picture.
3. Draw what you remember.

4 WHAT MAKES A HOME?

A HOME, INSIDE A HOME, INSIDE A HOME, INSIDE A HOME ...

How many homes can you draw? Draw them one inside the other.

Use different colors.

Try with your eyes closed.

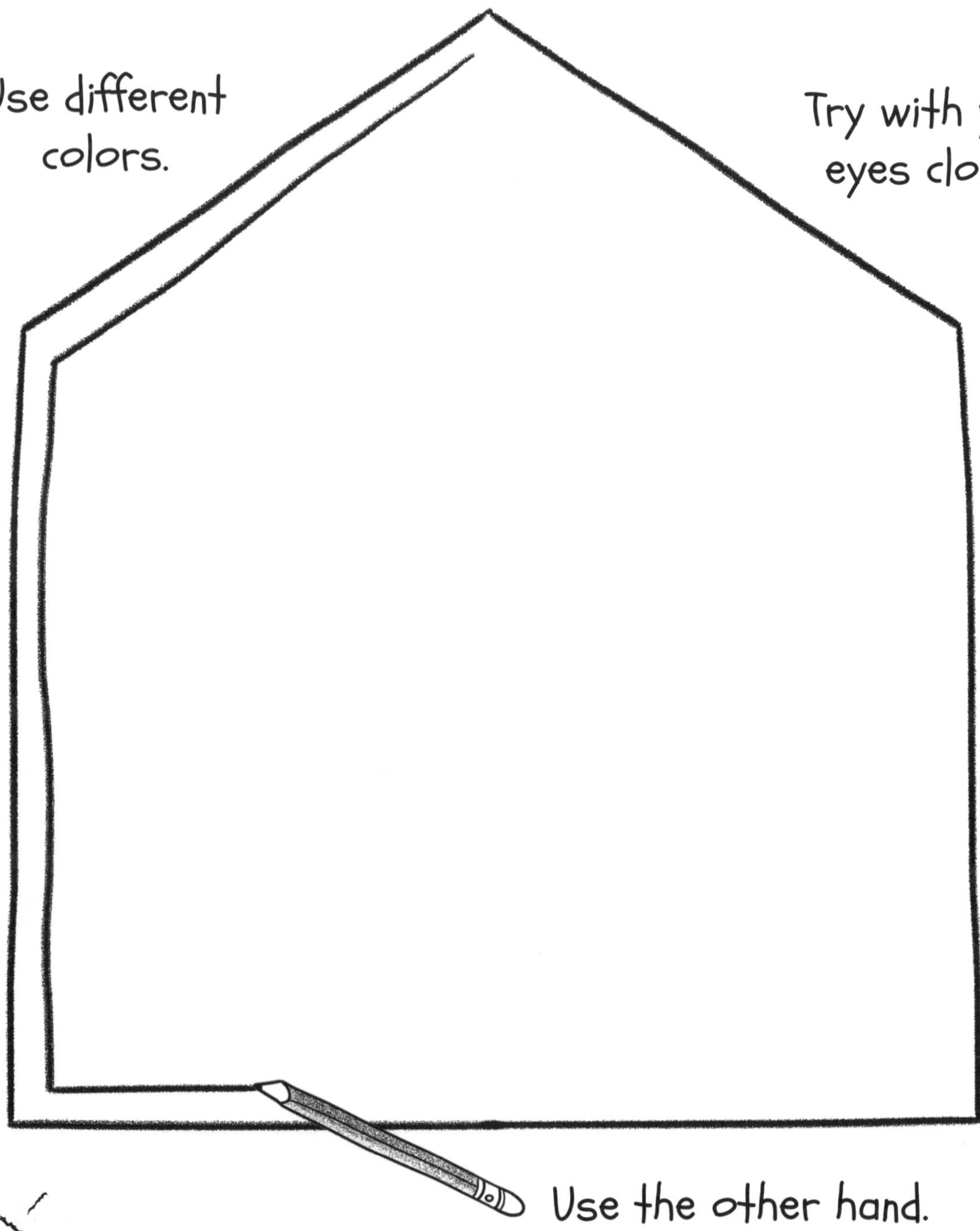

Use the other hand.

LOOK UP. WHAT DO YOU SEE?

Imagine you are lying in bed. Look up. Draw what you see.

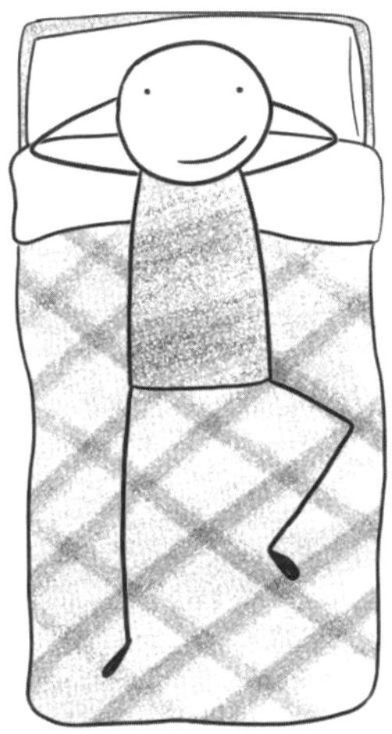

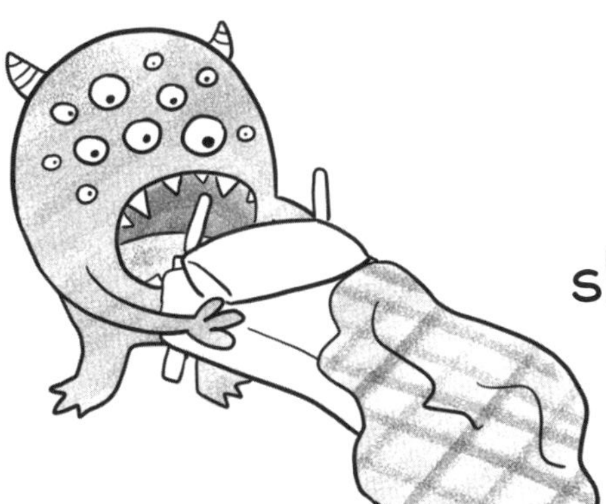

It can be anything: the stars in the sky, a bed-eating monster, an amazing pattern ... or just the ceiling.

SNAILS, SNAILS, SNAILS EVERYWHERE!

How many snails can you draw? Big, small, red, blue, green ...

HELP SNAIL, SPIDER, AND LADYBUG STAY DRY.

Draw where the friends go to stay dry.

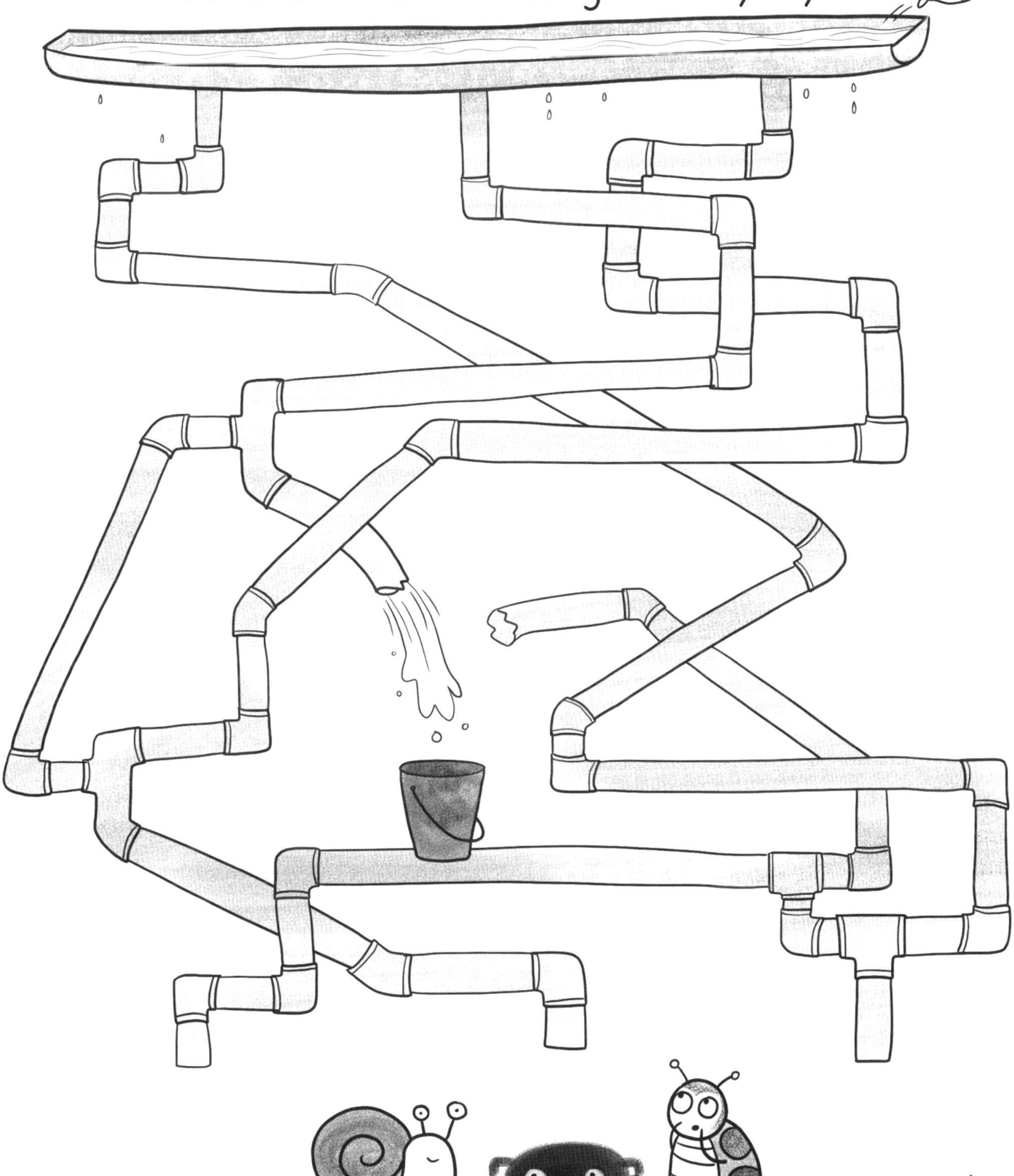

5 WHERE DO WILD ANIMALS BELONG?

Octopus is painting things he finds in his home. Find and color what he paints.

WHERE IS THAT ZEBRA?

COLOR IN WITH BLACK EACH SECTION THAT HAS A DOT. COLOR IN EACH SECTION THAT HAS A SQUARE WITH ANOTHER COLOR. CAN YOU FIND THE ZEBRA?

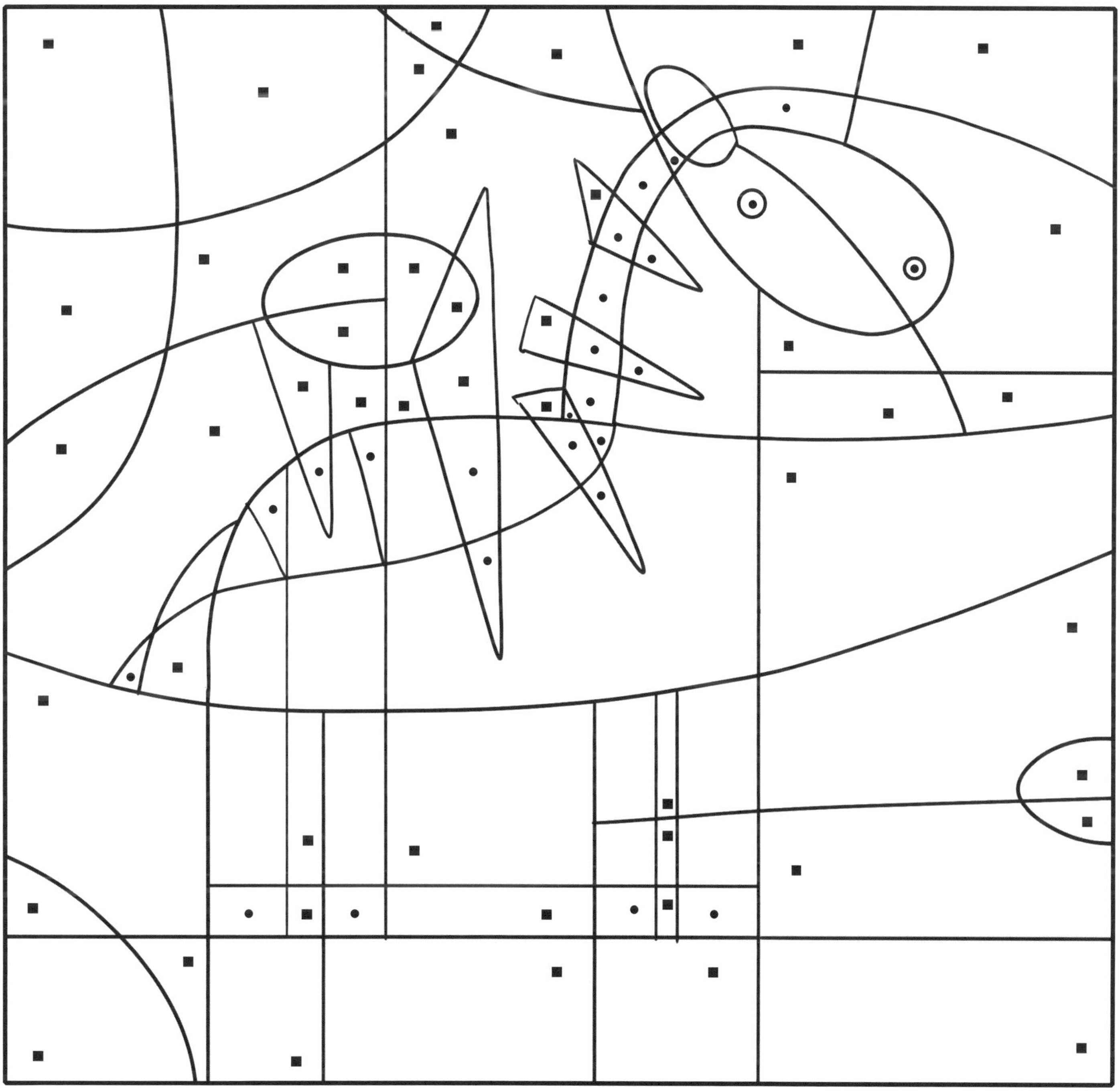

THE WHALE IS FULL

DRAW WHAT'S IN THE WHALE'S STOMACH.

WHAT COLOR IS THE PANDA?

OOOPS! THE PARROT IS NOW BLACK AND WHITE,
AND THE PANDA IS FULL OF COLOR.

6 WHAT CAN PEOPLE DO?

WHAT CAN YOU DO?

WRITE YOUR NAME ... DIFFERENTLY.

Which hand do you write with? Left or right?

Use the other hand. Write your name as many times as you can.

Write your name with your eyes closed.

Repeat as many times as you can.

Write your name backwards.

Repeat as many times as you can.

5, 4, 3, 2, 1!

LOOK AROUND OR IMAGINE. THEN, WRITE OR DRAW.

5 things you can see.

4 things you can touch.

3 things you can hear.

2 things you can smell.

1 thing you can taste.

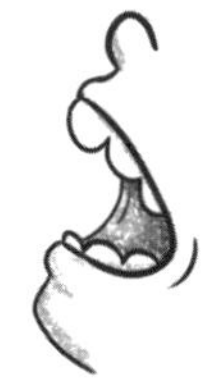

YOU CAN'T

WHAT CAN YOU DO?
USE PAPER OR PAINT TO COVER THE 'Ts.

I can't say and spell words backwards.

I can't speak English.

I can't draw.

I can't sing.

I can't dance.

I can't run.

I can't swim.

I can't read.

I can't ride a bike.

ADD SOME MORE THINGS YOU CAN'T DO.

CAN YOU DRAW? YES, YOU CAN!

LOOK AT EACH SQUARE CAREFULLY.
COPY THE PICTURE AND COLOR.

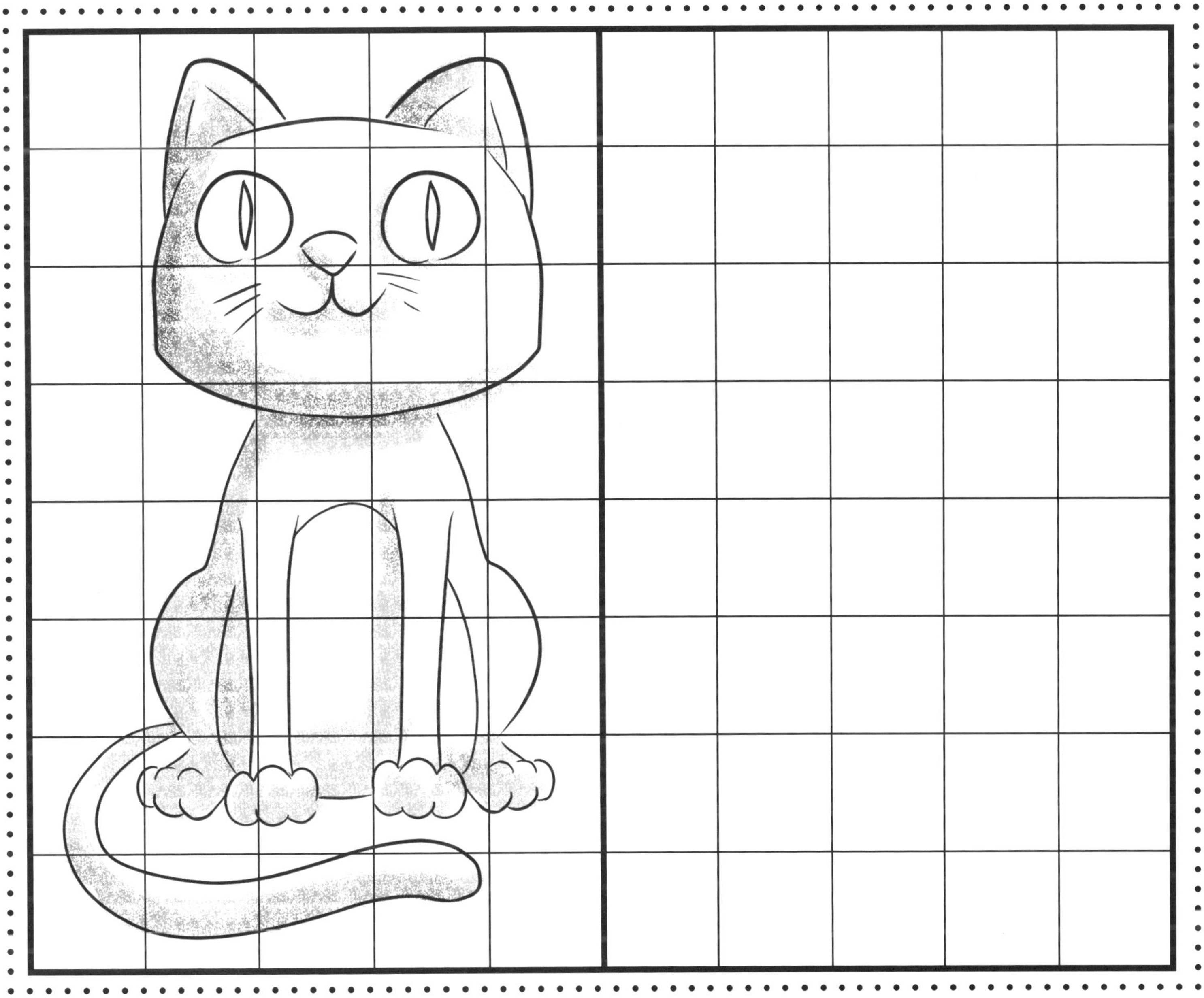

NOW DRAW SOME KITTENS HERE.

CREATIVE BLAST 2

TRY, TRY AGAIN

DON'T LIFT YOUR PENCIL.

Copy each picture. Don't go over the same line twice. And don't lift your pencil.

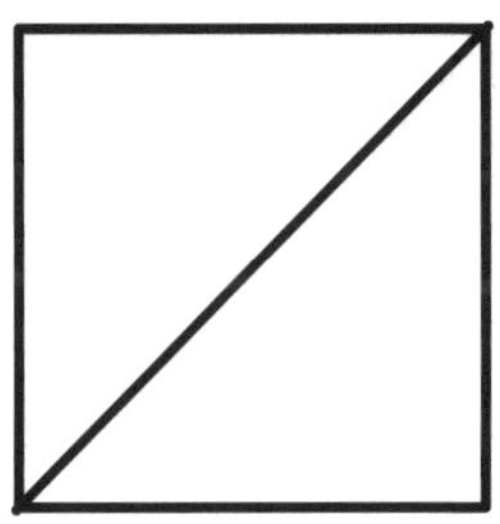

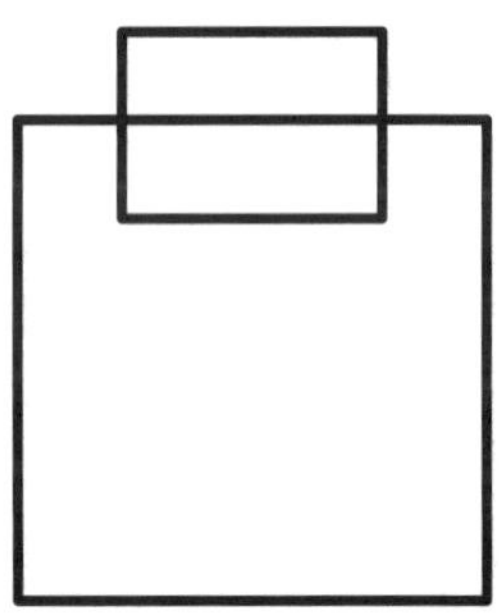

This one is difficult. Keep trying!

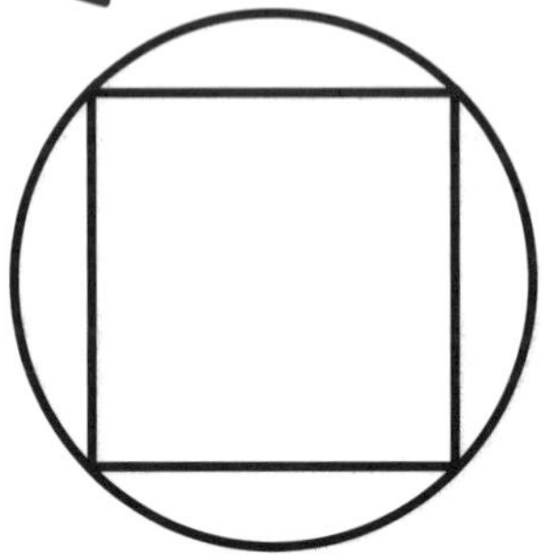

A DIFFERENT POINT OF VIEW

IT'S SO BIG!

What can the ant see?
Draw and color.

7 IS ALL FOOD HEALTHY?

BROCCOLI POPSICLE, ANYONE?

Make 4 popsicles, any flavor and shape that you want.

Is this one in the shape of a rocket?

What color is this one?

Maybe something salty and sweet?

Do you want to eat this one?

GET YOUR LUNCHBOX READY FOR SCHOOL.

FIT THE SANDWICHES IN THE LUNCHBOXES. DRAW THE PIECES ON EACH SANDWICH.

2 triangles

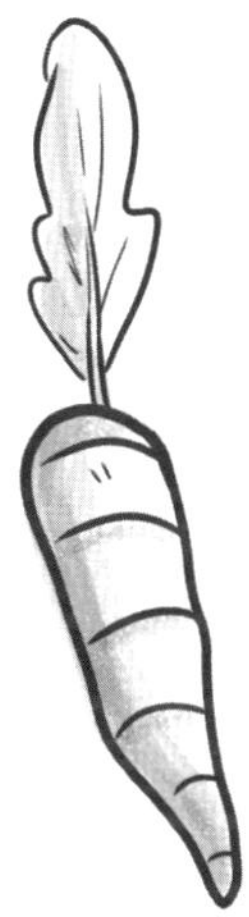

2 rectangles

4 squares

Draw your lunch here!

APPLE, APPLE, APPLE, APPLE, ORANGE?

FIND THE ITEMS THAT DON'T BELONG.

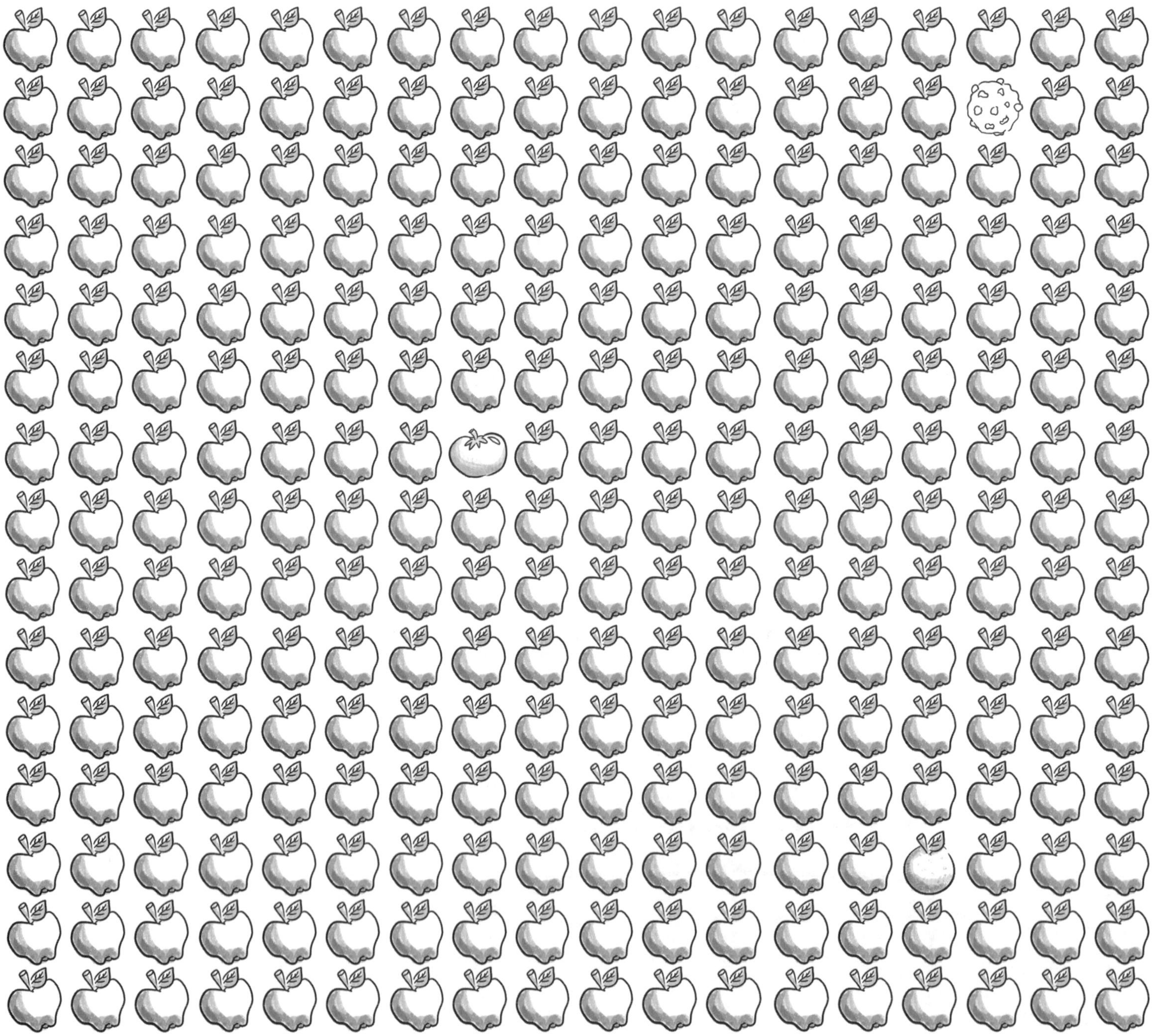

WATERMELONS ARE YUMMY, BUT THE SEEDS ARE YUCKY!

CAN YOU TAKE ALL OF THE SEEDS OUT OF THE WATERMELON?

Glue paper all over those yucky seeds.

Color in the watermelon.

8 ARE ROUTINES IMPORTANT?

PATTERNS AND ROUTINES

Draw what comes next in each pattern.

PATTERNS YOU MAKE WHEN YOU BRUSH YOUR TEETH

Close your eyes and imagine you are brushing your teeth. Answer and draw.

1. What patterns do you make when you brush your teeth? Do you make circles,

lines,

or zig-zags?

Draw the patterns here.

2. How many circles, lines, and zig-zags do you make? Draw them here.

THE EXCITING LIFE OF ANIMALS

What do these animals do all day long?
Look at the pictures and write or draw their routines.

Pandas ....all day long.

Sea turtles ....all day long.

Koalas..all day long.

What other animal has an easy routine?
What do you do all day long? Paint? Sing? Play soccer?
What other animal has a very difficult routine?

	My Guess	Total
As	10	8
Bs		
Cs		
Ds		
Es		
Fs		
Gs		
Hs		
Is		
Js		
Ks		
Ls		
Ms		
Ns		
Os		
Ps		
Qs		
Rs		
Ss		
Ts		
Us		
Vs		
Ws		
Xs		
Ys		
Zs		

HOW MANY LETTERS ARE THERE IN A WEEK?

Guess and check.

MONDAY 1

TUESDAY 2

WEDNESDAY 3

THURSDAY 4

FRIDAY 5

SATURDAY 7

SUNDAY 8

9 WHY DO WE WEAR DIFFERENT CLOTHES?

KEEP THE SNOWMAN WARM

It's not easy being a snowman. It's a very cold job. Draw clothes to help him stay warm.

EVERY DAY A DIFFERENT HAT

How many different hats can you draw?
Make sure they're all different.

SARI PATTERNS

Decorate the sari. Copy the pattern or make your own.

COLORFUL CLOTHES

Close your eyes. Imagine you're opening your closet. Think about all the colors you see. Draw the colors below.

DON'T FORGET YOUR SOCKS.

CREATIVE BLAST 3

QUESTIONS, QUESTIONS, QUESTIONS

WHAT IS YOUR FAVORITE?

Orange or blue?	Panda or koala?
Cheese or ice cream?	Snail or spider?
Soccer or tennis?	Jump rope or monkey bars?
Bike or car?	A or Z?
Banana or grape?	2 or 8?
Broccoli or carrot?	Hand or foot?
English or math?	Pen or pencil?
Singing or dancing?	Lion or mouse?
Octopus or shark?	! or ?

DON'T THINK, JUST ANSWER.

AROUND AND AROUND

PLAY WITH A FRIEND. FIND DICE AND ROLL THEM. MOVE YOUR COUNTER.

If you roll ...

- less than 7, roll again.
- more than 7, roll again. Go around again.
- exactly 7, you win!

HOW MANY TIMES DO YOU ROLL THE DICE BEFORE YOU GET 7?

THAT'S IT! YOU FINISHED!

LOOK BACK AT YOUR BOOK. WRITE WORDS, DRAW PICTURES, AND MAKE PATTERNS FOR EACH UNIT.

1

2

3

4

5

6

7

8

9